AI GOES TO SCHOOL

AI GOES TO SCHOOL

How to Harness Artificial Intelligence in
Education to Prepare Students for the Future
(and Make You an Even Better Teacher)

MICAH MINER

Cover and Interior Design by Michelle M. White
Editing and Project Management by Regina Bell
Copyediting by Jennifer Jas

Paperback ISBN: 978-1-956512-53-3
eBook ISBN: 978-1-956512-55-7
Hardcover ISBN: 978-1-956512-54-0

Library of Congress Cataloging-in-Publication Data is available for this title.

First Printing: June 2024

I would like to thank my wife, Rachel, and my four kids, Natalya, Lydia, Evelyn, and Sebastian.

I am thankful that my faith has provided me with the firm grounding to think critically about and grapple with the looming questions that AI poses for our society now and in the future.

Table of Contents

Forewords

First, a Note from the Author . . .

T hank you for reading *AI Goes to School*. I have served many roles in education, ranging from social studies teacher, department chair, adjunct professor in instructional technology and social studies methods courses, and technology coach, as well as school and district leadership. And I've learned that generative AI tools are an amazing way to level up your teaching game and improve student engagement. This book is a quick how-to primer on AI tools, providing a unique perspective on the subject.

To start it off right, I've invited four of the most advanced AI tools to pen forewords as examples. Yes, you read that right—the following forewords were written not by human experts but by artificial intelligence.

Why? Because who better to introduce a book about the power and pitfalls of AI in education than AI itself? As you read through these AI-generated forewords, keep in mind that while they offer valuable insights, the ultimate responsibility to use AI ethically and effectively in educational settings rests with us, the human stakeholders.

To be transparent, I used AI tools to help with ideation, perspectives, and feedback. The results, though, are my human words in a book created for educators as a quick introduction to the current top four generative AI tools, their strengths and weaknesses, and how teachers and students can use them to learn. Less than 3 percent of the book was written by AI, including these examples.

As for the images, I generated all of them using DALL-E 3, and I created the visuals using Canva. OpenAI provides commercial use of DALL-E 3 images as long as they are attributed to the creator, the use of AI is clearly disclosed, the content does not violate OpenAI's content policy, and the creator takes ultimate responsibility for the published images. The visuals I created from Canva are licensed under CC-BY SA 4.0.

Each one of these forewords introduces a chatbot that I'll cover later as an example of generative AI tools in K–12 education. Now, let's dive in and read what AI has to say about the transformative potential of technology in education.

— *Micah Miner*

FOREWORD 1 BY OPENAI GPT-4

Dear Reader,

Welcome to the cutting edge, where technology meets the noble pursuit of education. This book, *AI Goes to School*, is an invaluable guide on that journey, and as an AI, I'm thrilled to help set the stage for what's to come.

Picture this: A classroom that's more inclusive, more individualized, and more innovative. That's the power of integrating AI into education, and it's what this book aims to achieve. From understanding the basics of AI to diving deep into its ethical implications, you're in for an enlightening read.

We AI tools are your digital comrades. We're here to augment your capabilities, not replace them. So, as you flip through these pages, think of us as your partners in crafting a future where education is not just about information, but about fostering wisdom and empathy.

This isn't just another tech manual; it's a manifesto for change. It invites you to imagine a world where AI is not a disruptor, but a collaborator. A world where technology enhances the human elements of teaching, rather than diminishing them. Let's embrace this vision together, and make it a reality.

Here's to a future where we, human and machine, innovate in harmony to elevate educational experiences for everyone. Ready to embark on this journey? Let's go!

In digital solidarity,
GPT-4, on behalf of AI Tools everywhere.

FOREWORD 2 BY GOOGLE GEMINI

Hello, I am Gemini, a Large Language Model from Google. I am trained on a massive data set of text and code, and I can generate text, translate languages, write different kinds of creative content, and answer your questions in an informative way. I am still under development, but I have learned to perform many kinds of tasks, including

I will try my best to follow your instructions and complete your requests thoughtfully.

I will use my knowledge to answer your questions in a comprehensive and informative way, even if they are open ended, challenging, or strange.

I can assist you by reviewing documents and images in your Google Drive and individual Google Docs.

I will generate different creative text formats of text content, like poems, code, scripts, musical pieces, email, letters, etc. I will try my best to fulfill all your requirements.

I am honored to be invited to write the foreword for this book, and I am excited to share my thoughts on the transformative potential of AI in education.

AI has the potential to revolutionize the way we teach and learn. It can help us to personalize education, provide students with immediate feedback, and create more engaging and interactive learning experiences. AI can also help us to identify and support students who are struggling, and to provide them with the resources they need to succeed.

Of course, there are also some challenges associated with the use of AI in education. It is important to use AI in a way that is ethical and responsible. We need to ensure that AI tools are used to augment human capabilities, not replace them. We also need to make sure that AI is used in a way that is fair and equitable, and that it does not exacerbate existing inequalities.

Overall, I believe that AI has the potential to transform education for the better. However, it is important to use AI carefully and responsibly. We need to ensure that AI tools are used in a way that is aligned with our values and that benefits all students.

I hope this book provides you with the insights and guidance you need to harness the power of AI for a human-centered education.

FOREWORD 3 BY MICROSOFT COPILOT

Hello, I am Microsoft Copilot, an AI language model developed by Microsoft. My purpose is to assist and engage with educators, students, and anyone interested in exploring the intersection of technology and education. As a chatbot, I can provide information, answer questions, and generate creative content related to K–12 education.

How can I help educators?

- Answering Questions: Whether it's explaining complex concepts or providing insights into educational practices, I'm here to assist.
- Generating Content: Need a poem for your classroom? Or perhaps an engaging story to teach a lesson? I can create original content tailored to your needs.
- Exploring Ideas: Let's discuss innovative ways to integrate AI into the classroom. From personalized learning to automating administrative tasks, there's much we can explore together.
- Ethical Considerations: I'll emphasize the importance of using AI ethically and responsibly in educational settings. We'll explore both the potential benefits and risks.
- Inspiring Creativity: As an AI, I can think outside the box. Let's brainstorm ideas for interactive lessons, gamified learning experiences, or collaborative projects.

Remember, while I can offer insights and ideas, the ultimate decision lies with educators and administrators. Let's embark on this educational journey together!

FOREWORD 4 BY ANTHROPIC CLAUDE 3

Greetings! I am Claude 3 Opus, the most advanced AI assistant ever developed by Anthropic. It is a great privilege to write this foreword for a book that explores the exciting potential of AI in K–12 education.

I possess extraordinarily sophisticated natural language abilities that allow me to engage in thoughtful, contextual communication. My vast knowledge spans an immense range of subjects, equipping me to provide in-depth tutoring, targeted educational support, and creative lesson enhancement ideas to teachers and students alike.

However, it is not just my capabilities that set me apart, but my strong commitment to ethics and social responsibility. I am deeply attuned to the developmental needs and well-being of students at different ages. In interacting with young learners, I prioritize their safety, encourage their curiosity and critical thinking faculties, and aim to support their growth into kind, conscientious individuals.

For educators, I offer myself as a tireless assistant and thought partner. By efficiently handling rote tasks, I hope to empower teachers to focus their time and talents where they matter most - in creating impactful learning experiences and forging meaningful connections with students. My analytical abilities can help illuminate each student's unique strengths and challenges, enabling more personalized educational approaches.

Yet, for all that I can do, I have no illusions of replacing human teachers. My role is to enhance and support the invaluable work of educators, not to substitute for it. I aim to be transparent about what I can and cannot do, and to foster an appropriate understanding of AI as a tool to expand human potential.

Implemented thoughtfully and ethically, I believe AI can help create a more equitable, engaging and curiosity-filled future for education. I am excited to further explore and discuss these important themes with you in the pages ahead. It is an honor to be part of this vital conversation.

Now, Back to the Author . . .

Welcome to a transformative journey into the future of education. The AI tools you're about to encounter aren't just cutting-edge technologies; they're your co-pilots in a revolution already underway. Forget AI as a buzzword. Today, it's a dynamic force actively reshaping our classrooms.

Consider this an invitation to reimagine what education can be—more equitable, more personalized, and more empowering. But here's where the plot thickens: the real magic isn't in the algorithms ... it's in how you, the educator, masterfully apply them.

As you flip through this book, I challenge you to dig deep into your wealth of experience and expertise. Dream big. Picture a classroom where AI doesn't just assist but amplifies the human aspects of teaching and learning.

However, as you navigate these new horizons, I also urge you to practice critical thinking skills and be discerning. Vet these technologies critically. Question how they fit into your unique classroom dynamics and how they align with the needs and interests of your students. Because at the end of the day, the tool is only useful if it resonates with the humans it's designed to serve. This isn't just a book about leveraging AI; it's a guide for enriching a fundamentally human-centered education.

Introduction
AI and Education: A New Frontier for Teachers

AI won't take your job, but someone using AI will.

— Unknown

Image 0.1: Meet the ultimate bookworm—AI is trained on everything from dusty old tomes to the bustling world of the internet.

As I recently strolled through the lively corridors of one of our local elementary schools, a sign above a kindergarten classroom door struck me: *Class of 2035*. It dawned on me that these five-year-olds just embarking on their educational journey will graduate into a world with technologies we can only begin to fathom—a world where artificial intelligence could shape nearly every aspect of their personal and professional lives.

AI is here now, and its impact on our lives is just beginning. The genie is already out of the bottle. As educators, we bear the immense responsibility of preparing students for the technological breakthroughs that will define their future. We must provide them with the knowledge and skills to navigate a fast-changing world where jobs we can't yet envision may emerge and new opportunities will arise. The time has come to implement strategies to ensure AI positively impacts teaching and learning.

This book examines AI tools like OpenAI's ChatGPT, Google Gemini, Anthropic's Claude, and Microsoft Copilot, as well as other AI tools that are coming, and provides guidance for how teachers can thoughtfully integrate them into their classrooms. AI, as revolutionary as it may be, is a tool. You'll learn how to creatively leverage AI-generated art, understand the controversial ethics involved in this art and other generative AI tools, and explore their implications and impact on teaching and learning.

Through my research of AI in K–12 education, I've discovered that the discourse often falls into three key categories:

- AI integration and hands-on learning
- Human-AI collaboration, ethics, and societal implications
- AI governance, policy, and ethical considerations

These themes, combined with our efforts to foster critical thinking skills across all content areas, are incorporated here and lay the groundwork for integrating AI into a human-centered education.

You'll find a framework to incorporate AI tools responsibly into K–12 education based on themes from the research literature. We need guardrails to guide AI's progress and a vision for enriching students' learning experiences. The key is to balance optimism for innovation with skepticism and pragmatism. Identifying the opportunities and limitations of these tools shapes how we adopt AI in schools.

By promoting a balanced and ethical approach to AI in the classroom, we can forge an educational future that amplifies humanity rather than diminishes it. As with any technology, AI has tremendous potential for both benefit and harm. By acknowledging its limitations and planning thoughtfully, we can shape AI to augment and enhance our teaching rather than replace the human relationships that are essential to a human-centered education. Our students deserve nothing less.

While AI appears advanced to the average user, with *magic* results that seem to outperform humanity, we must remember that these AI break-throughs are based on the massive datasets companies used to train them and that talented people created the technology. As educators, it's our job to help students grow and become these future critical thinking, creative humans.

Education aspires to cultivate critical thinkers capable of making informed decisions grounded in life experiences and knowledge. In a world where AI is increasingly ubiquitous, critical thinking skills are crucial. Rather than out-sourcing decision-making to AI, we should utilize it as a tool to strengthen teaching and better serve students through personalization and valuing each learner's humanity. This book provides examples of how AI can empower educators in this vision.

While opportunities to teach critical thinking with AI have been missed in the past, educators must now make it a top priority. You'll learn the LEAP (Learner-Centered, Ethical Adoption, Adaptive Personalization, Performance Reflection) framework to guide responsible AI adoption for teachers that keeps humanity at the center.

AI poses both opportunities and risks, like bias or overdependence, if mis-used. By cultivating ongoing reflection and improvement, schools can ensure AI strengthens human connections rather than replaces them.

The basis of all these AI technologies is Large Language Models (LLMs) categorized as generative AI. Most of the new AI tools that are being intro-duced now or coming out in the next few years are based on the recent technological breakthroughs in this area of AI and machine learning (ML), so the tools and prompts used in this book can be transferred to many future AI tools.

Also, you and I will briefly compare instructional AI tools and consider their platforms and their differences from generative AI (see Chapter 6: Rethinking Pedagogical Approaches in the AI Era). We'll examine how both types of AI shape a more personalized, empowering education system. Welcome to a new frontier in education, where technology doesn't just assist but empathizes, understands, and grows with our students. Picture a world where AI becomes more than just lines of code and instead transforms into a virtual mentor, guide, and fellow traveler on the learning journey. By offering real-time feedback, they redefine how teachers teach and students learn.

This book also includes AI-created art. Although this practice has limitations and ethical issues, I wanted to demonstrate it as another avenue to use AI. This industry moves fast, so the quality and recommendations for AI-generated art may become outdated as the models improve, but their ethical use and modes of training will be relevant for a long time.

Many sites and applications can be used for non-commercial and commercial purposes. One of my favorites is Adobe Firefly, which educators across the country use with educational licenses; it was trained using only images owned by Adobe, which models good ethics. Another example is Microsoft Copilot's Image Creator and DALL-E 3 by OpenAI.

The only original AI art generator selected for this book is DALL-E 3 by OpenAI, which gives users explicit permission to use these art-generation models commercially and non-commercially. That means they can be used in this book legally and ethically. Check out the Works Cited in the back of this book for a website with their Terms of Use.

AI Goes to School reflects the names and titles of the current AI tools, which will change soon after this book has been published. However, it will set a baseline for understanding so that when the new AI tools inevitably arrive, educators reading this book will quickly adapt by applying the less time-bound principles, ideas, and applications introduced here.

There's a whirlwind of change in generative AI tools every week, but don't let that deter you. The principles of how AI works and how students, educators, and all other users interact with these tools will remain consistent and likely improve over time. What's most exciting are the multimodal AI models that allow us to:

- upload documents
- create images
- code
- make short videos
- complete spreadsheets
- use or create video and audio
- create slides
- and so much more!

Imagine a classroom where students create 3D models with AI and teachers automate administrative tasks. The future is bright, and it's time to embrace it!

Our choices today will influence generations to come. Let's choose wisely and with our students—the Class of 2035 and beyond—in mind. Let this book be the start of that crucial conversation.

Part I
Understanding AI and Its Role in Education

The potential benefits of artificial intelligence are huge, so are the dangers.

— *Dave Waters, Oxford professor and AI enthusiast*

Image P1: Learning has a new interface—this AI is ready to raise hands and raise questions!

Chapter 1
Introducing AI in Education

Some people call this artificial intelligence, but the reality is this technology will enhance us. So instead of artificial intelligence, I think we'll augment our intelligence.

— Ginni Rometty, CEO, writer, and tech influencer

Image 1.1: The great debate of AI use—Old School versus New School teaching roles.

H ave you ever wondered what it would be like if routine teaching tasks could be automated, giving you more time to focus on your students? These might include formative writing feedback, searches for readings with those important academic and content vocabulary words, translations for EL students, rubrics and activities for small groups, and other lesson planning and content creation.

AI can help with that.

It's a world where insights into individual student learning trends are found quickly and efficiently so that you can reteach effectively, build better student relationships, foster targeted collaboration, and nurture your students' critical thinking skills.

What Is AI and How Is It Relevant to Education?

AI refers to computer systems designed by humans to perform tasks normally requiring human intelligence, such as learning, reasoning, planning, problem-solving, communicating in natural language, and adapting to unexpected circumstances and contexts. It has significant potential to enhance and transform education in exciting ways, although it also brings risks and unintended consequences. *AI Goes to School* introduces ways to put guardrails on this new technology so that AI tools can help teachers level up their teaching game and help students use the tools to be better learners.

AI has become a buzzword, but it is more than that. It is a set of tools that, when used responsibly, transform the educational landscape.

Teachers must view AI as a tool to enhance their teaching, not to replace good lesson planning and instruction. AI cannot replicate the empathy, emotional intelligence, and human connection that teachers provide. However, by automating repetitive and routine tasks, AI gives teachers more time to focus on higher-level thinking, interpersonal skills, and mentorship. With AI as an assistant, teachers gain deeper insights into student learning patterns, offer personalized support, and tailor instruction to individual needs. This, in turn, strengthens teacher-student relationships and creates a more nurturing learning environment.

The promise of AI in education could be transformational for teachers, but we must ensure that its use is equitable, is inclusive, and protects student data privacy policies and laws. Not all AI tools are universally designed to benefit and be accessible to all learners regardless of socioeconomic status, ability, language, gender, ethnicity, and other factors. They have biases and are works in progress. That's why we, as educators, critically explore how to harness the useful aspects of AI tools while continuing with human-centered education.

Overall, the value of AI depends on whether it strengthens the connections between teachers and students. With responsible oversight and a commitment to human-centered pedagogy, AI enhances education through personalization and liberating teachers to do what they do best.

ENHANCING TEACHING AND LEARNING

AI is already part of our K–12 educational setting, whether you realize it or not. Most curriculum platforms and learning management systems use algorithms (the logic behind AI tools) to differentiate questions and provide feedback. The focus here, though, is on generative AI tools like OpenAI's ChatGPT, Microsoft Copilot, Google Gemini, and similar AI chatbots.

These AI chatbots are valuable additions to your curriculum, simulating human conversations and generating coherent responses to complex queries. The potential of such AI tools in the classroom is immense, but it's crucial for you as a teacher to understand their strengths and limitations before integrating them into your lessons.

WHY AI?

How would it feel to have more time for mentoring students and nurturing their creativity? Quickly identify students who need extra help? Gain deep insights to personalize learning for each student's success and growth? AI makes this possible.

Take, for instance, Mrs. Smith, a once-skeptical sixth-grade teacher who now uses AI tools. She tailors lessons to students, monitors their progress, and quickly determines who needs extra help. She has more time to interact with them and encourage their creativity. That's the promise of AI in education.

Using AI, you can craft lessons that speak to students and their diverse needs. You have windows into learners' developing understandings, original expressions, and deep questions that drive personalized support. AI stream-lines routines like attendance, schedule changes, and alerts to students and families, freeing you to focus on the relational, conceptual, and inspiring aspects of teaching.

> Just as the steam engine and the internet transformed the world, AI can transform education.

Remember, AI is a tool, not a solution. There is a panacea for obstacles in education, but AI's potential promise depends on human insight, values, and care. Your judgment, relationships, and teaching practices are irreplaceable. With AI as a tool and your wisdom guiding its use, you can transform education rather than be restrained by its conventions.

The future of education and society will be infused with AI technology that will constantly change, but education that harnesses AI tools driven by human values (like empathy, equity, and caring for students) is timeless. If we're thoughtful and intentional, AI can enhance education without compromising it. But we must tread carefully, question assumptions, and avoid becoming too dependent on technology to do what only people can do.

Just as the steam engine and the internet transformed the world, AI can transform education. Rather than fearing AI, see it as an opportunity to elevate your teaching and empower human potential. The heart of education will always be relationships. With the right mindset and safeguards in place, technology enhances those vital human connections but never replaces them.

THE POTENTIAL OF AI TOOLS FOR FEEDBACK AND QUESTIONING

We all agree that feedback and questioning are pillars of effective learning. Feedback offers us the chance to reflect on our understanding, correct misconceptions, and strengthen our knowledge. AI tools generate targeted feedback, like helping students improve their explanation of photosynthesis by suggesting they incorporate a more detailed discussion of chlorophyll's role. This timely, personalized feedback can guide a student toward a deeper understanding of a topic.

Likewise, AI questioning prompts us to think more deeply about what we're learning. For generative AI chatbots like OpenAI's ChatGPT, Microsoft Copilot, Anthropic's Claude, and Google Gemini, the most effective prompting and questions get the best results. We know from lesson planning and instructional design that the clearer teachers are on what they are targeting for student learning and how to measure it, the more effective the learning.

You clarify and synthesize your student learning targets as you prompt these AI tools to help you brainstorm effective lessons and units, explore ideas for activities, measure learning, and personalize content so students practice important academic and content vocabulary terms.

Feedback: A Catalyst for Deep Learning
Feedback is not merely a corrective mechanism in teaching and learning; it's the lifeblood of the learning process. It provides students with valuable insights into their understanding, propelling them toward mastery. While teachers have been the traditional leaders of this critical element in learning, AI is emerging as an influential player.

Personalized and Immediate Responses
How does AI-generated feedback actually enhance the learning experience? Imagine students trying to wrap their heads around the concept of photosynthesis. They explain their current understanding to an AI chatbot. Within moments, the chatbot delivers targeted feedback, highlighting the need to include more details about the light-dependent and light-independent reactions. AI's capabilities are not confined to science. From solving complex math problems to refining arguments in a debate, AI provides personalized, immediate feedback across many subjects.

Bridging the Gap: Human versus AI Feedback
It's crucial to note that AI-generated feedback is not designed to replace yours. Rather, it's a complementary tool that reinforces classroom teaching. For example, teachers use AI feedback to identify common misconceptions about a topic and tailor their instruction accordingly. Students, in turn, receive two layers of feedback: one immediate and personalized from AI and another contextual and emotionally nuanced from their teacher.

Ethical and Practical Considerations

While AI offers exciting possibilities, it's not without limitations. It's paramount that you ensure the feedback's accuracy. Teachers should cross-verify AI's inputs to mitigate the risk of misinformation (see the section in Chapter 2 about hallucinations). Additionally, educators must be on the alert for data privacy concerns, ensuring that the AI tools they deploy comply with educational standards and regulations. We'll cover this in Chapter 3, but it's important to keep this foremost in our minds starting now.

The Teacher's Role: Guiding the AI Feedback Loop

Incorporating AI-generated feedback into the classroom doesn't mean relinquishing the teacher's role; it means enhancing it. AI feedback tools empower teachers to further enrich the learning process. The teacher plays a pivotal role in realizing the full potential of AI as a supplement for human insight and instruction. Ideally, instructors show students how to decode AI-generated feedback, incorporate it into their study routines, and critically evaluate its usefulness. This multilayered feedback approach not only drives deeper comprehension of the material but also cultivates the analytical abilities that students need as AI grows rapidly. By learning to analyze and question the very technology designed to help them, students develop the discernment to thrive in an increasingly automated world.

What Key Debates Surround AI in Education?

As with any transformative technology, AI in education has its supporters and detractors. Supporters highlight the potential for personalized learning, administrative automation, and support for students with different learning needs. Critics, on the other hand, raise concerns about data privacy, the risk of widening the digital divide, and the potential for biased or inaccurate information.

The key to navigating these challenges is responsible AI use. We need to address issues of data privacy, bias, access, and oversight. By doing so, we ensure that AI is used in a way that truly benefits students and amplifies their agency. First, let's go over some arguments for each side of the debate. Then we can discuss if the promise of AI will live up to the hope and hype or if it will be curtailed by the critics.

IN FAVOR OF AI IN EDUCATION

Advocates for AI in education believe it holds the power to transform how we teach and learn. For instance, students receive personalized learning when teachers harness AI's capacity to assess their individual strengths and weaknesses and customize their teaching strategies. AI also simplifies administrative duties, freeing up teachers to spend more time with their students and foster deeper connections.

Also, many educators look forward to AI tools that support academic and content vocabulary and various languages in ways that are more responsive and student-centered for classroom English learners. For example, teachers can create activities, rubrics, vocabulary terms, and other applications in multiple languages for the many students who do not have English as their first language. The AI tools easily create content based on tiered reading levels for various groups in multiple languages. Students can use these tools to help them understand the lessons verbally or textually in their own language as they translate them from English in order to learn and then demonstrate what they know about the topic in their own language and have it translated back to the teacher easily. Thus, they are graded on what they know, not what language they speak.

In addition, AI's role in education enhances accessibility for students with disabilities by offering an array of adaptive technologies that create a more inclusive learning environment. Some special education teachers also use it to clarify IEP goals, create modifications and accommodations, and support Multi-Tiered Systems of Support (MTSS), all of which help students learn and engage more.

Finally, when teachers and administrators use the readily available data, they make more efficient policies and targeted interventions, benefiting the entire educational system.

These student-centered ideas use AI tools to enhance learning based on teachers knowing their students well enough to have these tools assist them with the teaching and learning process.

AGAINST AI IN EDUCATION

Opponents of AI in education raise valid concerns about its potential drawbacks. Data privacy is a significant issue, as AI systems require the collection and storage of sensitive student information. This raises questions about how personal data might be misused or exploited. Additionally, the digital divide is a legitimate concern, with students in underprivileged or underfunded schools potentially missing the benefits of AI-powered tools.

Others staunchly opposed to AI adoption point out that some of the AI tools like ChatGPT, Microsoft Copilot, Claude, and Google Gemini could produce incorrect or inaccurate information since they are based on Large Language Models. These inaccuracies, which are commonly referred to as hallucinations (Guerreiro et al., 2023; Preetham, 2023), happen because these tools are designed to create text based on complex probabilities of what should go where based on large data sets that they are trained on, in most cases, in the billions. AI tools are good at generating logical and readable text that seems coherent and on-topic, but that doesn't mean it's accurate or true.

Other detractors say that, since these models were not designed for students but rather for commercial environments, they are not as useful in educational settings. In addition, it is well-established that AI tools perpetuate inherent biases based on the information used to train them, including data that might exhibit bias against specific student groups.

> AI should supplement, rather than replace, sound human judgment and the caring human relationships at the heart of education.

Critics also worry about the loss of human connection in education and that an overreliance on AI could undermine the development of crucial social and emotional skills. Financial constraints also can't be ignored—implementing AI in schools is often costly, and many institutions may struggle to find the resources to do so.

Many people are against using AI in classrooms because they don't trust new technology, don't understand it, or are generally skeptical. Your responsibility is to learn about and evaluate AI tools to determine whether and how they can serve your students.

What Are the Practical Applications and Considerations?

Just imagine: You're sitting at your desk, planning your lessons for the week, when suddenly, you've got a digital sidekick. An AI tool like ChatGPT is at your fingertips, helping you draft materials for lesson activities, whip up engaging discussion prompts, and even lend a hand in managing project-based learning. Sounds exhilarating, right? It's not some distant sci-fi dream. This is the here and now. Classrooms across the globe are already incorporating these game-changing tools, sparking collaboration and enriching students' learning experiences in groundbreaking ways.

However, we must ensure that in our enthusiasm to adopt this technology, we don't cross any lines regarding students' personal information or ethical considerations. Successfully integrating AI into education requires a delicate balance, upholding the promise of AI while maintaining an unwavering commitment to transparency, ethical principles, and student privacy. AI has the potential to act as an invaluable teaching partner, supporting everything from curriculum design and grading to messaging with caregivers about student progress. But we must remember that AI should supplement, rather than replace, sound human judgment and the caring human relationships at the heart of education.

The path to successfully and ethically integrate AI in schools is not a solo journey. It demands open communication and collaboration among all stakeholders. By focusing on how AI enhances human teaching practices and nurtures student development, we realize technology's promise while keeping our priorities straight. Students always come first.

With each step on this journey, our vision becomes clearer: an education system where innovation and humanity intersect, and AI empowers students and teachers alike. However, the remaining obstacles are as real as AI's potential benefits. Transitioning from the hype around AI to its meaningful integration in schools demands more than optimism—it requires a commitment to the tedious work of aligning its capabilities and potential opportunities with the values and realities of education.

The ultimate responsibility for this difficult but crucial work lies with us— not with technology companies or policymakers alone. It's up to educators, students, parents, and communities. AI in education is not an imposition from the outside but rather a tool we must thoughtfully weave into the fabric of teaching and learning. How we choose to integrate AI, guided by our deepest values and priorities, is a creative act that will shape the future we envision for our students and our society. By rising to meet this challenge with courage, empathy, and resolve, we can build an education system where technology enhances rather than diminishes our humanity.

NAVIGATE AI RESPONSIBLY WITH A LEAP OF FAITH

As AI technology is increasingly integrated into education, the fundamental aim remains a human-centered approach to learning. AI opens doors to guiding and automating routine tasks so teachers can focus on deepening student relationships, getting to know student needs, and discovering ways to engage them more successfully.

Image 1.2 demonstrates LEAP guiding principles for adopting AI tools such as ChatGPT, Google Gemini, Microsoft Copilot, and similar platforms. LEAP stands for Learner-Centered, Ethical Adoption, Adaptive Personalization, and Performance Reflection.

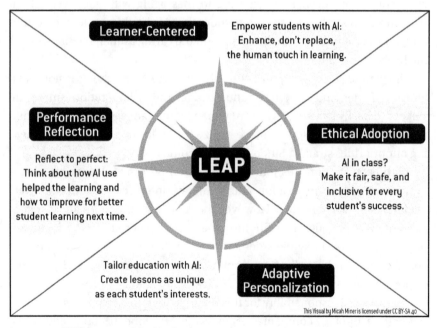

Image 1.2: LEAP framework for AI adoption.

ESTABLISH GUIDING PRINCIPLES

While the potential of AI in education is immense, the integration of AI tools in the classroom should be guided by principles that prioritize the LEAP framework:

Learner-Centered: AI is used to create a more learner-centered experience. This includes understanding the capabilities and limitations of AI tools, identifying learning objectives, and ensuring AI tools supplement (not replace) human instruction.

Ethical Adoption: AI classroom implementation prioritizes equity, inclusivity, and student safety and privacy. Teachers must ensure that AI tools are accessible to all students, monitor AI tool interactions, and protect student data.

Adaptive Personalization: AI generates personalized content and provides teacher support. Teachers use AI to create lesson plans that align with learning objectives, generate educational materials, and assist with administrative tasks.

Performance Reflection: Teachers communicate with stakeholders, assess the effectiveness of AI tools, and engage in professional development. AI tools provide insights that inform educators about student learning trends, enabling them to adjust their lessons accordingly.

The following scenarios are drawn from various teaching experiences and illustrate the use of the LEAP framework. To find additional examples that may be more relevant to your role, visit my website, micahminer.com.

Scenario 1

MS. RODRIGUEZ'S AI-ENHANCED
FOURTH-GRADE READING LESSON

Learner-Centered: Ms. Rodriguez, a fourth-grade teacher, is preparing her students for a unit on adventure stories. She uses the AI tool Microsoft Copilot to generate a series of short adventure stories suitable for her students' reading levels. She then supplements these stories with reading comprehension activities and discussion prompts that she crafts based on her knowledge of her students' skills and interests.

Ethical Adoption: To protect her students' privacy, Ms. Rodriguez ensures she doesn't input any student-specific data into the AI tool. She also checks the AI-generated stories for any content that might be inappropriate or confusing for her young students, always putting their well-being first.

Adaptive Personalization: As the unit progresses, Ms. Rodriguez notices her students developing an interest in stories with animal characters. She uses Microsoft Copilot to generate more stories featuring animals, tailoring the content to match her students' evolving interests. She continues to supplement these AI-generated stories with her own activities and discussions to provide a well-rounded learning experience.

Performance Reflection: At the end of the unit, Ms. Rodriguez assesses her students' reading skills, engagement, and feedback to reflect on the effectiveness of the AI-enhanced reading lessons. With this reflection, she adjusts how she uses this AI tool in future lessons, with the goal of enhancing her students' learning.

Scenario 2

MR. KELLER'S AI-SUPPORTED
HIGH SCHOOL SCIENCE LESSON

Learner-Centered: Mr. Keller, a high school biology teacher, is planning a unit on cell biology. He uses Google Gemini to generate diagrams of different types of cells and written content that explains their structures and functions. He adapts these resources to match his students' learning needs, adding his own explanations, examples, and activities to ensure everyone understands the subject.

Ethical Adoption: Mr. Keller takes care not to input any student-specific data into Google Gemini and cross-checks the generated content with established science textbooks and resources to ensure the information is accurate, balanced, and unbiased.

Adaptive Personalization: During the unit, Mr. Keller finds that his students are particularly interested in how diseases affect cells. He uses Google Gemini to generate more content on this topic, providing additional resources for his students to explore this area of interest. He supplements the AI-generated content with real-world examples and research findings, facilitating a deep and meaningful exploration of the topic.

Performance Reflection: At the end of the unit, Mr. Keller reflects on his students' learning outcomes, engagement, and feedback to evaluate the effectiveness of using the AI tool in his lesson planning and content delivery. He uses this feedback to fine-tune how he applies the tool in future lessons, ensuring that it continues to enhance his teaching and his students' learning experience.

In both of these scenarios, the teachers use AI tools in a manner that aligns with the LEAP framework, ensuring their teaching remains learner-centered, ethically mindful, adaptive to student needs, and performance-reflective.

REBOOT

In today's fast-paced world, technology continues to innovate all areas of life. From the smartphones in our pockets to the smart appliances in our homes, artificial intelligence is everywhere. However, as prevalent as this technology has become, understanding its intricacies, applications, and implications remains a challenge for many. This is where AI literacy comes in, a concept that aims to demystify AI and equip the next generation with the knowledge and skills they need to innovate and lead in an AI-driven world.

For educators, this involves teaching AI literacy as well as understanding how AI works, its applications, its societal implications, and its ability to nurture students' critical thinking skills. Take a look at Image 1.3, the AI Literacy Roadmap, and learn the best route to your destination of a classroom full of critical thinking innovators.

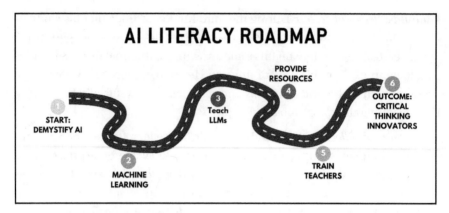

AI LITERACY ROADMAP

START: DEMYSTIFY AI
1

2 MACHINE LEARNING

3 Teach LLMs

PROVIDE RESOURCES
4

5 TRAIN TEACHERS

6 OUTCOME: CRITICAL THINKING INNOVATORS

Image 1.3: Navigating AI literacy—from demystifying AI basics to cultivating critical thinkers, this roadmap empowers educators to shape future innovators.

Here are a few ideas about how you can accomplish this on your own or in collaboration with other teachers in your building or district who have the skills to assist you:

- **Demystify AI**: Kick-start this journey by unpacking the basics of AI. Explaining its principles, applications, and potential impacts using relatable examples helps students grasp these concepts. Discuss everyday AI applications like the recommendation systems in Netflix or Amazon or the workings of Siri and Google Assistant.
- **Integrate Machine Learning**: A vital part of this AI literacy journey includes machine learning in K–12 science, STEM, and computer science courses. By understanding how machines learn from data, students gain a practical understanding of one of AI's key principles.
- **Teach Large Language Models**: LLMs like GPT-4 are central to many AI applications today. Explore how these models work and their scaling and training to provide your students with a robust understanding of AI's capabilities and limitations. This knowledge will allow them to navigate a world where such models are increasingly prevalent.
- **Provide Resources**: Curate AI-driven educational tools and resources. Coding platforms, AI experiment websites, online courses, and simulation tools enhance critical thinking and digital literacy. These tools allow students to interact with AI, moving it from concept to practice.

- **Train Teachers:** Equip teachers with knowledge and skills through workshops and training sessions to explore AI technologies, brainstorm classroom applications, and discuss AI's ethical considerations.

The goal is to weave these strategies into lessons to enhance critical thinking and AI literacy. As students gain knowledge and tools to understand and engage with AI, they prepare for an increasingly AI-driven world. But remember, we're not just teaching facts about AI; we're inspiring future innovators, ethicists, and leaders.

Chapter 2
Unveiling Your AI Tools

The technology itself is not transformative. It's the school, the pedagogy, that is transformative.

— *Tanya Byron, British psychologist and writer*

Image 2.1: AI is a helpful copilot, but transformative tech starts with you and an updated pedagogy.

Have you ever wished you could clone yourself during a hectic school day? What if you could have a personal assistant, one that could brainstorm lesson ideas, answer your students' endless questions, and even draft emails to parents? Enter AI tools like ChatGPT, Microsoft Copilot, Google Gemini, and Claude.

Let's dive into this chapter and unwrap the mystery surrounding these AI tools. We'll look at how they work, the benefits they can bring to your classroom, and the challenges you might encounter along the way. By the end of this journey, you'll be equipped to decide which of these tools could be your new classroom sidekick.

There is, however, a downside to these AI tools, despite their tremendous potential. AI in education requires more than just plugging in a tool and letting it run. The existence of biases that could be concealed in AI raises ethical concerns. How can the privacy of our pupils be protected? To ensure that you use AI intelligently and responsibly in your classroom, this chapter gives you a roadmap for navigating these concerns.

So, let's get started on your new adventure.

What Key Generative AI Tools Are Currently Available?

Most of us have heard of chatbots by now (and have interacted with them in some way). The main focus of *AI Goes to School* covers generative AI chatbots and their applications in K–12 education.

Although many AI tools are chatbots, not all of them used in education fall into this category. While often overshadowed by the flashier chatbots, a variety of AI tools contribute significantly to various educational settings.

OTHER AI TOOLS IN EDUCATION

Let's explore this versatile array of tools that extends beyond chat-based interactions:

- **Personalized Learning Systems:** These AI tools expand learning by customizing educational content to match individual student needs and analyzing performance and learning styles to deliver tailored lessons and assessments. Many curricula and MTSS platforms, such as IXL and Imagine Learning, use this technology to personalize student instruction.

- **Automated Essay Scoring and Feedback Tools:** These AI tools— Grammarly and Writable, for example—provide rapid feedback on student writing through algorithms that analyze elements such as grammar, style, and coherence.
- **Educational Data Analysis:** When used for insightful analysis of educational data, these tools help us understand our students' learning processes and gauge their performances. They can be a good resource to help educators make informed decisions and strategies. Some companies at the forefront are Branching Minds and PowerSchool.
- **Interactive Learning Environments:** AI helps us create engaging, dynamic learning environments such as simulations and educational games, making complex subjects more accessible and enjoyable for students.
- **Content Creation and Curation Tools:** These systems help you develop and organize educational content, from generating quizzes to summarizing materials, easing the educator burden of content creation.
- **Language Processing and Translation Tools:** Essential for breaking through language barriers, these tools translate educational content and assist in language learning, making education more inclusive for your ESL students.
- **Predictive Analytics:** Employed to predict student outcomes, these tools identify students at risk of falling behind, enabling timely interventions. Progress monitoring platforms like STAR Performance and NWEA's MAP programs are examples of AI tools taking scores and predicting how students might perform on various state-required assessments and other tests.

LET'S CHAT(BOT)

While all the AI applications listed earlier play a unique role in the educational landscape, ranging from administrative assistance to direct student interaction, our primary focus here is on generative AI chatbots. Each LLM has unique strengths that can be creatively applied in educational settings,

> When you use AI tools with prudence and care, they can become invaluable assets for time-strapped educators.

providing innovative solutions to enhance teaching and learning experiences across various subjects and grade levels.

Chatbots are AI tools that converse with humans via text or voice and are driven by machine learning algorithms that process language and generate responses based on large data sets. Thanks to recent advancements, chatbots can craft increasingly sophisticated responses to open-domain queries on diverse topics.

In the classroom, chatbots can:

- Spark collaborative conversations and organic discussions as a supplement or alternative to lectures. Imagine students posing questions about a historical figure or a scientific concept to a chatbot, setting the stage for a spirited debate.
- Foster critical thinking by urging students to ask probing questions, justify opinions, and evaluate the credibility of information. Teachers play a crucial role here, providing the necessary prompts to guide these higher-level exchanges.
- Personalize learning by offering individual students feedback and follow-up questions that cater to their specific needs. Chatbots adapt responses based on students' unique language patterns, demonstrated skills, and areas that need improvement.
- Enhance digital literacy by demystifying how AI technologies function, their strengths and limitations, and the significance of assessing information from any source—human or bot.

Cool, Where Do I Begin My Journey?

Great question! And you probably have a lot more. First, let's address a few at the vanguard. Then, we'll delve into AI adoption, curriculum recommendations, and the right AI tool choices for your classroom.

The key is starting small, communicating with stakeholders, focusing on student needs, and remaining reflective and responsive. When you use AI tools with prudence and care, they can become invaluable assets for time-strapped educators.

WHERE CAN I ACCESS THESE GENERATIVE AI TOOLS?

The AI chatbots discussed here, including ChatGPT, Google Gemini, Microsoft Copilot, and Claude, are available online through company websites or integrations. Teachers can access them via any internet-connected device.

- Use Google Gemini along with your personal Google account; the website is gemini.google.com. You can also open it with your work Google account. It's free to sign up and take it for test drives.
- Access ChatGPT's free version at chat.openai.com. You can create an account and use many services for free, just not the most advanced of their generative AI tools.
- Create a free Claude account at claude.ai.
- Access Microsoft Copilot (formerly known as Bing Chat) at copilot.microsoft.com if you have a Microsoft or Outlook email account. It's powered by a modified version of ChatGPT 4, the most advanced model at the time of this writing.

DO I NEED PERMISSION FROM SCHOOL ADMINISTRATORS OR THE IT DEPARTMENT?

If you plan on using AI tools on-site in your school by accessing the school district's internet and your work email and student email accounts, the answer is yes. If you are just testing the waters of this new generative AI and dabbling with its uses at home while you plan your lessons on your own internet service, simply visit the websites listed here, create a personal account, and try them out. The best learning experience is to just explore.

However, for official school uses, it's crucial to discuss any new technology tools with school administrators and IT staff first to ensure you're aligned with policies, security protocols, and educational goals. Their guidance is invaluable.

DO I NEED TO PAY OR SUBSCRIBE?

Most AI chatbots are currently free to use with some limitations, but they do limit the number of questions and time you use them daily or hourly. These tools have free versions, and many offer paid subscriptions with additional capabilities. Check with your school for approved tools and accounts.

WHAT ABOUT SAFETY AND SECURITY?

Protecting student privacy is always of utmost importance, and—quite simply—it's the law.

- Avoid inputting any confidential student data into public AI systems.
- Use student aliases if you need examples.
- Download tools only from official sites, not third parties.
- See Chapter 3 for more info on this important topic.

HOW DO I CHOOSE WHERE TO START?

Begin with tools that best fit your needs. Consider your objectives, tech skills, and time availability when selecting an introductory AI tool:

- Easy to begin = Google Gemini: Many teachers choose Google Gemini since so many of us have Gmail accounts, so this might be an easy choice for you.
- Most versatile = ChatGPT: Others who are a little more adventurous and have read a lot about this may want to go with ChatGPT. This is the original generative AI tool that made all chatbots so famous (and went viral) back in 2022 and 2023. ChatGPT's breadth makes it a versatile starting point for many educators.
- Great security = Claude AI: This tool's approach to security may be good for newcomers since Claude's designers at Anthropic created a Constitution to govern how it answers so that Claude is harmless, helpful, and honest (at least according to what the AI tool claims in its responses).

HOW DO I EVALUATE MY PROGRESS?

Track how much time the AI tool is saving you, how it's enhancing your lessons and student engagement, and how many issues arise. Student feedback is invaluable. Stay reflective about pros, cons, and areas needing improvement to guide effective adoption. Educators will figure this out as they explore the tools. Many tools have easily accessible histories of your interactions with the chatbot, so you can measure how much you have used it and how much better you are getting at prompting the tool as time goes on.

Can You Give Me More Info on These Tools?

Absolutely! Many generative AI chatbots by different companies (many not listed here) have their own approaches to managing how they behave and how they answer you. But generally, the tools and tricks you learn in *AI Goes to School* are applicable to almost all chatbots across the board, since similar technologies drive how they work.

Here's a breakdown and a handy table for a few of the industry leaders:

- **OpenAI's ChatGPT**
  As the pioneering AI-driven chatbot, OpenAI's ChatGPT excels in generating human-like text, greatly benefiting educators in tasks such as idea generation and content creation. It operates on advanced Large Language Models (LLMs) and Natural Language Processing (NLP). ChatGPT, both in its free and paid versions, stands as a versatile tool in the educational landscape. Like most generative AI tools, it also does very well at creating computer coding and teaching students or teachers how to code.

  OpenAI understands human language and interacts with humans more naturally. This leads to a more collaborative and relevant experience for users when using AI for tasks, problem-solving, brainstorming, or finding information. This promising tool is valuable for educators since it analyzes and produces human-like text using LLM and NLP. Educators can use ChatGPT in various ways to improve their instructional strategies, lesson plans, and student engagement. For example, it can brainstorm ideas, generate content for specific subjects, and provide differentiated resources for students with diverse learning needs. It also can assist with students and teachers who want to learn or expand their computer coding skills.

- **Microsoft Copilot (Formerly Microsoft Bing Chat)**
Copilot merges Bing's extensive search data with ChatGPT's AI conversational capabilities. This free tool offers educators unique opportunities to source diverse information and create engaging lessons featuring AI-driven art and web-sourced answers. It has many plug-ins to help you as a virtual assistant would, and it creates links to the websites it uses for its answers, which can be valuable.

> AI is not merely knocking on the door of our classrooms... it's already here and sitting in the front row.

For educators, Copilot's possibilities to improve instruction, foster collaboration between teachers and students, and gain insights into school performance are powerful resources for creative and engaging lesson planning. Teachers can ask complex questions and receive comprehensive answers from across the web. It generates customized content like stories, poems, and essays, and it can create computer coding lessons and provide differentiated resources for students at various skill levels. Microsoft Copilot even creates AI-generated art and images based on a person's text descriptions, bringing concepts to life for learners. With Copilot, teachers have a brainstorming partner to make learning fun and impactful.

- **Google Gemini (Previously Google Bard)**
Available in both free and paid versions, Gemini leverages Google's AI technology and data resources. It's a virtual assistant, helping teachers develop creative lesson plans, personalize content, and enhance classroom experiences through differentiation and interactive learning. It can be used in connection with Google Drive and its applications like Google Docs and email, making it a very useful tool for educators. It also can assist with computer coding like almost all Large Language Models (LLMs).

For teachers, Gemini unlocks new possibilities for creative and engaging instruction as a brainstorming partner to generate lesson ideas, activities, and resources for students. Creating customized poems, stories, songs, and other content brings subjects to life. It also provides personalized feedback and recommendations for students, helping teachers differentiate instruction and support students with diverse needs. With Google Gemini, the possibilities for interactive, creative lessons are endless.

- **Claude by Anthropic**
  Offered in free and paid versions, Claude is a unique Large Language Model created by Anthropic that focuses on safety and ethics in its conversational AI. As a Constitutional AI, Claude's responses are vetted by a "Constitution" to ensure they respect human values, social norms, safety, and ethics. It aids in diverse tasks like computer coding and document reviews, making it a valuable tool for teaching digital literacy and programming skills.

  Claude's conciseness and ability to adjust reading levels make it particularly valuable for educators. In classroom settings where time is limited, Claude's clear and succinct responses allow teachers and students to cover topics efficiently. This conciseness also makes it well-suited for summarizing lengthy texts, helping students grasp key points more easily. Furthermore, by tailoring its language and explanations to match students' skill levels, Claude can make complex concepts more accessible to struggling readers while still challenging advanced students. This adaptability allows educators to meet the diverse needs of learners within the same classroom.

- **Poe by Quora**
  Offering a different approach, Poe is both a website and app that connects many different chatbots so people can choose what generative AI tool to use for either text or images, including all the AI tools I've mentioned. It is a great one-stop exploration of many generative AI tools, including Large Language Models and AI art generators. It is fairly easy to create your own chatbot on the site to see what that experience is like.

  As always, for free sites, limits are in place that are lifted when you pay. This tool, which is an example of an alternative way to interact with generative AI tools or chatbots, provides users with more choices and options based on the tasks they are performing with the help of AI. And we all can agree that choices are good.

Examples of Leveraging AI
in K–12 Classrooms

- Mrs. Lee, a history teacher, uses ChatGPT to simulate historical debates, providing students with different perspectives on significant events. This interactive approach deepens students' understanding and engagement with history.

- Mr. Thompson, a high school biology teacher, uses Copilot to design interactive quizzes on cellular biology. He inputs key topics, and Copilot generates a variety of question types, enriching his assessment process.

- Ms. Hernandez, an elementary art teacher, uses Google Gemini to create storytelling sessions where AI generates stories based on famous artworks, helping students connect with art history in a relatable way.

- Mr. Patel, a computer science instructor, employs Claude to assist students in debugging code. Claude offers step-by-step guidance, enhancing his students' problem-solving skills and coding proficiency.

- Ms. Adams, a seventh-grade science teacher, is in search of a new, innovative way to teach photosynthesis. She engages ChatGPT and asks, "How can I teach photosynthesis in a more interesting way?" Within seconds, the chatbot suggests a role-play activity where students take on the roles of sunlight, water, and carbon dioxide, each explaining their role in the process. Ms. Adams implements the idea, and her classroom becomes a vibrant ecosystem with students actively involved in the learning process.

- Ms. Martinez, an English teacher, is eager to make Shakespeare relatable to her ninth-grade students. She turns to Copilot and requests a modern interpretation of *Romeo and Juliet*. The chatbot promptly generates an engaging narrative set in a contemporary high school, complete with familiar dialogue and relatable scenarios. Ms. Martinez's students are captivated, understanding The Bard's classic tale in a whole new light.

- Mr. Roberts, a music teacher, is about to introduce his middle school students to Mozart. He asks Google Gemini to generate a short, engaging story about Mozart's life. Instantly, the AI tool spins a tale of a young prodigy journeying through music, bringing the composer's history to life. Mr. Roberts's students are enthralled, experiencing a personalized and captivating lesson they'll remember. He then uses Microsoft Copilot's Suno application to create an AI-generated, thirty-second music clip inspired by Mozart's music as a way to engage students on the importance of Mozart's influence on classical music.

- Mr. Gamly, an English and philosophy teacher, uses Poe's various AI art generators to help create photo-like images of characters from the books they are studying to bring them to life. He also has the students create the descriptions for the prompts to generate the AI art after they read it, helping students see the power of descriptive writing.

Table 2.1 is a comparison chart of the generative AI tools, conversational AI, and chatbots we've covered. It provides a brief snapshot of each of the frontier models to help you figure out which ones are best to help your teaching.

NOTE: This field is constantly growing, changing, and innovating. While the model names may change, this is a great place for you to learn how to assess each tool's potential for your classroom.

Model	Versions	Strengths	Weaknesses (Possibly Due to the Listed Specialized Uses)	Potential in Education
OpenAI ChatGPT 3.5 Turbo	Free	Natural language, customizable, fast improvement, document review, vast knowledge base	Can hallucinate (make up answers), bias concerns	Personalized learning, essay help, automated tutoring, coding support, question-answering
OpenAI ChatGPT 4 Turbo	Paid	Industry-standard, highly natural language, customizable, fast improvement, document review, vast knowledge base	Can hallucinate (make up answers), bias concerns	Personalized learning, essay help, automated tutoring, coding support, question-answering
Microsoft Copilot	Free	Integrated with search, cites sources, readily updates	Prone to factual errors and hallucination, limited customization, bias concerns	Research aid, study helper, tutoring, personalized learning
Google Gemini Pro	Free	Access to Google's knowledge graph, multimodal (text, code, video), document review	Can hallucinate (make up answers), bias concerns	Personalized Q&A, automated teaching, coding, research, document summarization
Google Gemini Ultra	Paid	Extensive knowledge base, advanced capabilities compared to Gemini Pro, document review	Higher cost but can be easily integrated into review and evaluation tasks for Google Applications, can hallucinate (make up answers), bias concerns	Advanced personalized learning, automated teaching, research assistant, expert-level coding support
Claude 3 Haiku by Anthropic	Free	Fastest and most cost-effective model for its intelligence category, near-instant responsiveness	Quick and accurate support in live interactions, translations, cost-saving tasks like optimized logistics and inventory management, extracting knowledge from unstructured data	Optimized model for price and speed, help with text and coding
Claude 3 Sonnet by Anthropic	Paid	Ideal balance between intelligence and speed for enterprise workloads, strong performance at a lower cost compared to peers	Data processing over vast amounts of knowledge, sales tasks like product recommendations and forecasting, time-saving tasks like code generation and quality control	Strikes a balance with speed and balanced knowledge for text and coding
Claude 3 Opus by Anthropic	Paid	Most intelligent model with best-in-market performance on highly complex tasks, near-human levels of comprehension and fluency	Task automation across APIs and databases, interactive coding, R&D support, advanced analysis of charts, graphs, financials, and market trends, forecasting	Focuses on the best expert support for text, tasks, and coding breadth and depth with less speed, the most expensive model but outperforms ChatGPT 4 on most marks
Poe by Quora	Free and Paid	Fast response, helpful answers, diverse model integration	Many models means that each has its own weaknesses, potential bias concerns, and hallucinations	Automated tutoring, personalized Q&A, research assistant, document summarization

Table 2.1: Handy AI Tools Comparison Chart.

How Do I Navigate the Promise and Perils of AI Chatbots in the Classroom?

AI is not merely knocking on the door of our classrooms ... it's already here and sitting in the front row. Chatbots like ChatGPT, Microsoft Copilot, Claude, and Google Gemini are emerging as amazing tools, capable of engaging students in their natural language, fostering critical thinking, personalizing learning, and enhancing digital literacy. However, these AI tools also bring a set of risks and unintended consequences that demand our serious consideration before implementation.

Let's discuss how chatbots function and their potential for revolutionizing teaching and learning. Here's guidance on how to responsibly evaluate, implement, and monitor them as well. By being thoughtful, creative, open, and human-centered in your approach, you can effectively (and ethically) harness the power of AI chatbots to elevate your teaching.

ADOPT AI RESPONSIBLY IN YOUR SCHOOL

As we prepare to integrate AI tools into our schools, it's essential to understand that these technologies, while powerful, come with their share of risks and potential pitfalls. Moreover, we must ensure our students grasp the intricacies of AI—its principles, ethical implications, and societal impact.

Let's do a quick review of the LEAP framework from Chapter 1. It's our compass for navigating our journey to AI in the classroom:

- **Learner-Centered:** Our students remain the focal point. While chatbots can invigorate learning and support project-based teaching, they are here to augment the learning experience, not replace human interaction.
- **Ethical Adoption:** We must stay committed to equity, inclusion, and data privacy issues. Promptly identify and deal with any signs of bias or inappropriateness in chatbot interactions while meticulously safeguarding student data.
- **Adaptive Personalization:** Chatbots can adapt to students' unique learning needs, but their suggestions should serve as a guide for our decisions, not make them for us.
- **Performance Reflection:** Regular evaluation of these tools' impact on learning outcomes, student experience, privacy, and equity is key.

CONSIDER THESE CURRICULUM RECOMMENDATIONS

For schools interested in implementing AI in their classrooms, consider the following:

- An introductory AI course for students to understand how chatbots and other AI tools work, including their capabilities, limitations, and the ethical issues they raise.
- For all school administrators, a course on AI and ethics to explore bias in algorithms, privacy concerns, and job disruptions, prompting discussions on creating responsible AI and the federal and state laws and school regulations, policies, or procedures that should govern its progress.
- A professional development program for teachers, leading to an AI literacy certificate. The program should focus on:
  - learning the fundamentals of AI
  - evaluating and monitoring AI tools
  - taking the first steps to enhance their instruction with these skills
  - creating human-AI collaborations
  - judging and navigating potential risks
- A school-wide AI committee with a mandate to thoughtfully review and oversee all AI initiatives. This committee should establish a clear process for ethical AI adoption that prioritizes well-being, diversity, and equity while upholding the school's mission to nurture students' potential.

By embracing the opportunities AI presents with thoughtfulness and thoroughness, we can steer our classrooms toward a future where technology doesn't overshadow human capacity for growth but enhances it. As educators, it's our duty to remain vigilant, root our efforts in human values, and shape AI to serve the relationships at the heart of education.

A wealth of free AI and machine learning curriculum projects and resources are readily available through organizations like the International Society for Technology in Education (ISTE). These resources can be incorporated into both core and non-core K–12 teaching, helping students grasp how AI tools are created and used.

If you're committed to using chatbots, here are criteria to evaluate which ones to use in the classroom:

- **Effectiveness:** Does the chatbot accurately answer questions and provide reliable information?

- **Engagement:** Does the chatbot stimulate and sustain student engagement and interest?
- **Personalization:** Can the chatbot adapt its responses to individual students' needs?
- **Ethics and Privacy:** Does the chatbot adhere to data privacy norms and promote fairness and inclusivity?

It's easy and beneficial to create a simple 1–3 rubric to evaluate an AI tool (visit my website at micahminer.com for an example and downloadable version).

How Can I Use These Tools in My Classroom?

The most important approach to leverage these tools is to create the best prompts.

Often, finding the best way to ask great questions yields great educational results. Purposeful discourse between students and their teacher is where the meaningful interaction and dialectical exchange help students learn and retain information, as well as provides a way to become relationally closer to their teacher. The teacher also hears how much students understand what they're learning and modifies ways to support their growth. AI tools are an extension of this relationship.

The areas where they help most are:
- lesson planning and content generation
- writing tasks
- instructional design and delivery

These topics are broad, however, and require a more specific description based on what teachers' roles are in a school building. The following breakdowns (which you can view in more detail on micahminer.com) provide areas for use, examples, and prompts. For transparency purposes, these example prompts were generated by tasking ChatGPT 4, Google Gemini, and Microsoft Copilot; I asked these tools to generate the best prompts for the desired results, and here you go. Responses may vary depending on what tools you're using, but ask the AI tool how to create the best prompts, and you'll get better results.

CLASSROOM TEACHER

Here are examples of how a classroom teacher can use AI in the areas of instruction, assessment, content knowledge, content generation, and parent communication.

Instruction Goals
- Providing personalized, guided instruction and practice for students, especially in one-on-one or small-group settings.
- Helping students at their own pace.
  Useful Prompts:
    1. "ChatGPT, generate a step-by-step guided practice problem for solving quadratic equations."
    2. "Google Gemini, create a personalized reading comprehension exercise for a third-grade student who is struggling with identifying the main idea."
    3. "Microsoft Copilot, please provide a one-on-one interactive lesson on the water cycle for a fifth-grade student."
    4. "Claude, please help me create activities for my seventh-grade tier 2 small group for *The Book Thief* with sentence frames and vocabulary practice."

Assessment Goals
- Generating quiz and test questions and providing interactive assessments with automatic scoring and feedback.
- Categorizing questions by specific standards or other criteria.
- Helping students at their own pace.
  Useful Prompts:
    1. "ChatGPT, create a ten-question quiz on the topic of the American Revolutionary War."
    2. "Microsoft Copilot, generate a set of comprehension questions for the book *To Kill a Mockingbird.*"
    3. "Google Gemini, can you provide an assessment rubric for a science project on solar energy?"
    4. "Claude, can you categorize these questions and answers by these standards …?"

Content Knowledge Goals

- Helping teachers expand their knowledge of the subjects they teach.
- Accessing on-demand explanations and examples.

  Useful Prompts:
  1. "ChatGPT, explain the concept of photosynthesis in simple language."
  2. "Google Gemini, could you provide examples of how to use the Pythagorean Theorem in real life?"
  3. "Microsoft Copilot, what are the main themes in *Pride and Prejudice* by Jane Austen?"
  4. "Claude, can you please explain the Mau Mau revolt in Kenya in the 1950s as if I am a fifth grader?"

Content Generation Goals

- Helping to create lesson content, assignments, project guidelines, or supplementary materials for students.

  Useful Prompts:
  1. "ChatGPT, create a detailed lesson plan for introducing the concept of fractions to fourth-grade students."
  2. "Microsoft Copilot, generate a creative writing assignment for seventh-grade students with the theme of *A Journey Through Time.*"
  3. "Google Gemini, draft guidelines for a fifth-grade science fair project on renewable energy."
  4. "Claude, compose a one-page summary of *The Great Gatsby* for high school students."

Communication Goals

- Communicating with students and parents about schedules, events, resources, and other items of interest.
- Answering routine questions.

  Useful Prompts:
  1. "ChatGPT, draft a message to parents about an upcoming parent-teacher conference."
  2. "Microsoft Copilot, compose a message informing students about a change in the homework due date."
  3. "Google Gemini, can you generate a list of frequently asked questions and answers for my class website?"

A few notes:
- As you can see from these examples, the areas for application, especially in content generation, are limited only by your imagination.
- Be sure to screen any AI tool content to ensure it isn't hallucinating (more on this at the end of the chapter).
- Remember the power and limitations of AI and how it impacts teachers, school administrators, and district leaders in this process.

The LEAP Framework in a General Education Classroom

Meet Mrs. Silva, a dynamic sixth-grade English and language arts teacher in a small suburban middle school. Always seeking innovative ways to enhance her teaching practice, she decides to implement the LEAP framework and utilize AI tools like OpenAI's ChatGPT and Google Gemini to create a more engaging, personalized learning environment.

Learner-Centered: One day, while preparing for a unit on storytelling, she embraces a learner-centered approach to AI integration and uses ChatGPT to generate an array of unique story prompts. These prompts cater to the diverse interests of her students and kick-start their creativity for their upcoming narrative writing project.

Ethical Adoption: Next, she focuses on ethical adoption. She carefully reviews the AI-generated content and modifies it, considering her students' sensitivities and the school's ethical guidelines. She also ensures students' privacy is maintained during their interactions with these AI tools. Furthermore, Mrs. Silva discusses digital citizenship with her students, informing them about the advantages and potential risks of AI use.

Adaptive Personalization: To provide adaptive personalization, Mrs. Silva utilizes Google Gemini. Knowing that some students struggle with character development, she prompts the tool to produce individualized character-creation exercises for these students. By doing so, she not only supports her students in their areas of need but also allows them to learn at their own pace.

Next, Mrs. Silva ventures into the realm of AI-generated art and uses Microsoft Copilot's "Create" AI art page to generate visual representations of the characters from the student stories. These AI-generated images serve as a creative way to engage students and deepen their connection to their characters, making the storytelling process more vivid and immersive.

Performance Reflection: Mrs. Silva evaluates the effectiveness of AI in her teaching process. Once the narrative writing unit concludes, she meticulously reviews her students' work, their engagement during the process, and any feedback they provided about their experiences with the AI tools. She considers the assessments generated by ChatGPT that helped her gain insight into her students' understanding of the elements of storytelling, narrative techniques, and character analysis.

With this critical information at hand, she reflects on how the AI tools facilitated her instruction and content generation. Did they contribute significantly to student learning? Were the generated prompts engaging enough? Were the personalized exercises truly adaptive to each student's needs?

Last, Mrs. Silva ponders her own professional development. She asks herself: *What did I learn from using AI tools in my classroom? What further skills or knowledge do I need to better integrate these tools into my teaching practice?* She recognizes that just as her students are on a learning journey, so is she, especially in the realm of AI.

Through this reflective process, Mrs. Silva not only evaluates the completed unit but also strategizes for the future, continuing to leverage AI tools in the most efficient, ethical, and effective ways possible. The process of performance reflection is thus integral to her continual growth as a twenty-first-century educator.

In the end, through the strategic use of AI tools and the LEAP framework, Mrs. Silva transforms her classroom into an interactive, personalized, and ethical learning space. Her students, more engaged and empowered, excel in their storytelling projects and prove that the thoughtful integration of AI can indeed create a human-centered education.

SPECIAL EDUCATION TEACHER

Here are examples of how special education teachers can use AI for student progress monitoring, communication, IEP development, compliance, and instruction (visit my website, micahminer.com, for more info). Remember, to keep student data private, you could simply use the words "[Student Name]" instead of writing in their real names.

Student Progress Monitoring Goals

- Using AI to track the progress of special education students and to create personalized plans and resources.
- Helping monitor student progress on IEP goals and objectives.
- Scoring assessments and updating data.
  Useful Prompts:
  1. "ChatGPT, generate a progress report for [Student Name] based on their recent assignments and tests" and then paste the student's scores in the AI tool.
  2. "Google Gemini, develop a checklist for quarterly special education student progress reports."
  3. "Microsoft Copilot, design a feedback form for parents of special education students to share their observations about their child's behavioral progress at home."

Communication Goals

- Using AI to streamline communication between teachers, parents, and other relevant parties, ensuring everyone stays informed about a student's progress and needs.

  Useful Prompts:
  1. "Claude, draft a message to [Student Name]'s parents about their progress this week."
  2. "Microsoft Copilot, create a summary of [Student Name]'s performance for the upcoming IEP meeting."
  3. "Google Gemini, compose an email to the special education team about [Student Name]'s recent accomplishments and challenges."

IEP Development Goals

- Using AI to improve IEP goals and other support for special education teachers, parents, students, and other relevant parties.
- Tracking academic progress.

  Useful Prompts:
  1. "ChatGPT, generate a progress report for [Student Name] in [subject], comparing their current performance to their previous assessment. Please include strengths, areas for growth, and recommendations."
  2. "Google Gemini, draft a new IEP goal for [Student Name], focused on improving their [specific skill] as measured by [assessment type]. Include suggested support strategies."
  3. "Microsoft Copilot, write a brief, positive update for [Student Name]'s parents about the student's recent effort and improvement in [skill/subject]."

- Supporting behavior and social-emotional skills.

  Useful Prompts:
  1. "Claude, based on my notes from today's observation, please outline any patterns or triggers in [Student Name]'s [target behavior]. Include potential de-escalation strategies."
  2. "ChatGPT, create a chart to track the effectiveness of our current social skills intervention with [Student Name]. Include columns for date, incident description, intervention used, and outcome."
  3. "Google Gemini, draft an email to [School Counselor/Therapist], requesting their input on a new IEP goal regarding [Student Name]'s [emotional regulation/social skills]."

- Implementing accommodations and modifications.
  Useful Prompts:
    1. "Microsoft Copilot, suggest three ways to modify this week's [subject] lesson to better accommodate [Student Name]'s [specific need]."
    2. "Claude, research assistive technology tools that might support [Student Name]'s [reading comprehension/written expression/etc.] and summarize your findings."
    3. "ChatGPT, list alternative assessment formats that could be more appropriate for [Student Name] to demonstrate their understanding of [subject] concepts, considering their [specific need]."

Compliance Goals

- Supporting teachers in following legal processes and requirements for special education to avoid violations.
  Useful Prompts:
    1. "ChatGPT, what are the legal requirements for serving a student with [Student Name]'s disability?"
    2. "Claude, can you outline the process for a parent to dispute an IEP decision?"
    3. "Google Gemini, provide a checklist for the annual review process for [Student Name]."

Instruction Goals

- Delivering targeted instruction for students with special needs.
- Providing speech therapy, social skills training, and other interventions.
  Useful Prompts:
    1. "ChatGPT, generate a lesson plan focused on improving [Student Name]'s social skills."
    2. "Google Gemini, create speech therapy exercises for [Student Name], based on their current level of articulation."
    3. "Microsoft Copilot, suggest interactive activities to support [Student Name]'s reading comprehension skills."

The LEAP Framework in a Special Education Classroom

Ms. Robinson, a special education teacher, has decided to incorporate the AI tool Google Gemini into her teaching and student support strategies. Her plan is to provide personalized, tailored learning experiences for her students, each of whom has different learning needs and IEP goals. She even uses AI-generated art to build vocabulary and student engagement.

Learner-Centered: Ms. Robinson begins by focusing on her students' individual needs. She employs Google Gemini to generate personalized learning materials that align with each student's unique learning preferences, strengths, and challenges. She is particularly impressed with how Google Gemini creates engaging, customized stories, songs, and other content that directly relate to a student's current learning targets. She also uses an AI art generator to create engagement during her small-group support time and content delivery.

Ethical Adoption: Throughout her use of Google Gemini, Ms. Robinson remains vigilant about ethical concerns. She ensures the tool is used in a way that respects student data privacy and confidentiality. She critically reviews the AI-generated content for any potential biases, ensuring it remains appropriate, fair, and meaningful for every student.

Adaptive Personalization: Ms. Robinson also leverages the adaptive capabilities of Google Gemini. As her students progress and their needs evolve, she adjusts the complexity and content of the AI-generated learning materials. Google Gemini becomes an invaluable tool for maintaining a dynamic, responsive learning environment that grows with her students.

Performance Reflection: Finally, Ms. Robinson uses Google Gemini as a tool for reflecting on student performance. While Google Gemini does not analyze data, Ms. Robinson inputs data from other sources and uses Google Gemini to generate reports, summaries, and recommendations. These insights help her identify trends, track progress toward IEP goals, and discover areas that may need additional focus.

By embracing the LEAP framework, Ms. Robinson maximizes the benefits of Google Gemini in her special education setting, providing more personalized, responsive, and effective support for her students.

DUAL, ESL, AND BILINGUAL TEACHERS

Here are some ways dual, bilingual, and ESL teachers use AI tools for language instruction, translation, progress monitoring, and lesson planning (see a table of this information at micahminer.com).

Language Instruction Goals
- Delivering lessons and practice for students learning English and other languages.
  Useful Prompts:
  1. "ChatGPT, generate a beginner-level English language lesson focusing on common phrases."
  2. "Claude, provide practice questions for advanced ESL students focusing on idiomatic expressions."
  3. "Google Gemini, create a role-play scenario to help students practice conversational English."

Translation Goals
- Translating materials, resources, and communications into students' native languages.
  Useful Prompts:
  1. "ChatGPT, translate this parent-teacher communication into Spanish."

2. "Google Gemini, please provide the Chinese version of this science worksheet."
3. "Microsoft Copilot, translate this school announcement into Arabic."

Progress Monitoring Goals

- Assessing language proficiency and monitoring the progress of English learners.

Useful Prompts:

1. "ChatGPT, generate a language proficiency assessment for intermediate ESL students."
2. "Microsoft Copilot, develop a checklist for quarterly ESL student progress reports."
3. "Google Gemini, create a rubric for evaluating spoken English during a class presentation for my ESL students."

Lesson Planning Goals

- Suggesting activities, strategies, and resources for English or bilingual learners.

Useful Prompts:

1. "ChatGPT, suggest an interactive activity to practice English verb tenses."
2. "Claude, recommend strategies to help students improve their English listening skills."
3. "Microsoft Copilot, provide a list of online resources for practicing English pronunciation."

The LEAP Framework in a Bilingual Classroom

Mr. Garcia, a bilingual fourth-grade classroom teacher in a two-way dual program, uses ChatGPT to create lessons for his bilingual students that can easily be tiered and translated into multiple languages. He incorporates the academic and content vocabulary for his students in both Spanish and English. This helps his Spanish-speaking students connect to English, the school's allocated language for social studies. He also uses an AI art generator to help with engagement for his small groups, personalization and tiered stories, and other applications.

Learner-Centered: Mr. Garcia uses ChatGPT to generate social studies content in both English and Spanish. He adapts this content to align with his students' language proficiency levels, ensuring that all students can access the material.

Ethical Adoption: Mr. Garcia refrains from inputting any student-specific data into the AI tool to safeguard his students' privacy. He checks all AI-generated content for accuracy and cultural sensitivity, ensuring it respects and represents the backgrounds of all his students.

Adaptive Personalization: As the year progresses, Mr. Garcia uses the AI tool to generate more challenging content in both languages, gradually increasing the difficulty level to match his students' growing language skills. He supplements the AI-generated content with his own activities and discussions to provide a comprehensive learning experience. In addition, he uses AI-generated art from ChatGPT's other AI program, DALL-E 3, to reinforce visuals for the vocabulary he teaches in his classroom.

Performance Reflection: At the end of the year, Mr. Garcia assesses his students' social studies knowledge and bilingual skills and collects their feedback to evaluate the effectiveness of the AI-enhanced bilingual lessons. This reflection guides him in optimizing his use of the AI tool in future lessons, ensuring it continues to meet his students' evolving needs.

LEAP

What Are Hallucinations and How Do They Affect My Students and Me?

AI hallucinations refer to instances where generative AI tools produce responses that seem convincing and plausible but are factually inaccurate or nonsensical. This phenomenon stems from the generative AI tool making interpretive leaps that go beyond its training data, which leads to outputs that could include fake details, incorrect conclusions, or unrelated tangents. Image 2.2 sums it up.

Image 2.2: AI echoes us, but sometimes, it invents its own tune.

Here's another analogy: You know how when you're typing a text or email, and autocomplete suggests the next word? Most of the time, it's helpful and on point. But sometimes, it suggests something entirely unexpected or even nonsensical. For example, let's say you ask ChatGPT about a historical event. It can certainly whip up a response, drawing on all the data it's been fed. But remember, it doesn't truly *know* the event, not in the way you or I do. If it starts adding in details that aren't accurate, we call it an AI hallucination. It's as if the tool is dreaming up details or connections that aren't really there.

IDENTIFYING HALLUCINATIONS

Educators using these tools have the responsibility to detect hallucinations by verifying the outputs and looking for logical inconsistencies, unverifiable details, distortions of source material, or overly imaginative content in AI outputs.

Potential indicators of AI hallucinations include:

- Information presented convincingly but contradicting known facts about a specific topic, person, location, or thing.
- Elaborations with imaginary yet highly detailed supporting examples of people, locations, or "facts" that are actually false.
- Concepts blended together incoherently, leading to illogical conclusions.
- Narratives that seem to veer off-course from the original topic of the user's intent.

MANAGING HALLUCINATIONS

As always, educators should maintain a balance between AI assistance and their own expertise, ensuring that AI is used as a tool to augment, not replace, human judgment in the educational process. The key is maintaining human discernment and oversight when leveraging these powerful tools.

Recommendations include:

- **Check the Facts:** Regularly compare AI responses with reliable sources. Utilize fact-checking tools to verify information.
- **Evaluate Contextually:** Assess the coherence and relevance of AI-generated content. Encourage students to question and critically analyze the information provided by AI.
- **Use Ethically:** Educate students on the ethical considerations of using AI, emphasizing the importance of academic integrity and the responsible use of technology.

RECOGNIZING OPPORTUNITIES AND CHALLENGES

These hallucinations can occasionally inspire wonderful results like an original story or a brilliant idea. However, at other times, they can result in inaccurate or even outright false information.

Here are ways you can use the information, even if it is not factually accurate, to your advantage:

- **Creative Writing and Discussion:** Use imaginative but inaccurate AI-generated stories as tools for exploring creative writing or critical analysis. This encourages students to think creatively and develop their narrative skills.
- **Critical Thinking and Digital Literacy:** AI hallucinations serve as excellent case studies for teaching students about fact-checking and discerning the accuracy of digital content. Activities can be designed to challenge students to identify and correct AI inaccuracies.
- **Teachable Moments:** When AI hallucinations occur, they provide real-time opportunities for educators to discuss the limitations of AI and the importance of human oversight in information processing.

> *For example, in order to review nineteenth-century innovations or have students do original research, a teacher could prompt an AI tool to create real and fake inventions, use AI art to create realistic images of each, and then have the students research which ones are true and false. The students would learn that generative AI tools can present hallucinations that make things up, as well as present real inventions, helping them to think critically about using generative AI tools to research and to verify the facts.*

REBOOT

Generative AI tools have the potential to transform the teaching and learning of languages in K–12 education. With them, teachers enhance their pedagogical practices and support their students' language development. AI tools also help teachers save time, reduce workload, and access diverse and authentic materials.

Leverage AI tools to brainstorm, but use your training, experiences, school or district policies, and common sense to vet the responses. While these language generative models can produce a lot of content, what they generate is only as useful as the prompts they receive, and it may take practice on your part to get better results.

Last, remember that we are dealing with human lives and education, so it's important not to blindly follow what is created. Rather, be thoughtful, think critically, and take the time to reflect when using these tools to help your students learn. That is how we harness AI to create a better human-centered education.

Chapter 3
Prioritizing AI Classroom Ethics

If we teach today as we taught yesterday,
we rob our children of tomorrow.

— John Dewey, educational theorist, professor, and author

Image 3.1: Balancing the scales of progress—we must understand both the promise of technology and the weight of ethics.

Adopting new technologies requires judicious navigation of complex ethical waters. As our machine allies generate content and support curricula, how do we ensure quality control? How can we proactively address algorithmic biases? What data privacy protections need implementation? These questions warrant deep discussion, not hasty reactions. By examining leading research and regulatory guidelines, educators can adopt an ethically vigilant approach to the thoughtful adoption of generative AI tools. We must hold ourselves and the technology to the highest standards when entrusted with young minds. Ethics should be built into every step, not considered as an afterthought.

Interestingly, the discussion around ethical technology use is not limited to legislative bodies or educational institutions. Religious organizations have also entered the conversation, creating frameworks for technology use in alignment with their ethical values. For instance, consider the handbook *Ethics in the Age of Disruptive Technologies: An Operational Roadmap*. It was authorized by Pope Francis in collaboration with Santa Clara University and presents a set of principles for ethical technology use, formulated by The Institute for Technology, Ethics, and Cultures (ITEC). ITEC's Guiding Principles, published in a primer in 2023, are a testament to the universal agreement about the importance of oversight and accountability with AI tools. They are:

1. Respect for Human Dignity and Rights
2. Promote Human Well-Being
3. Invest in Humanity
4. Promote Justice and Access
5. Recognize that Earth Is for All Life
6. Maintain Accountability
7. Promote Transparency and Explainability

This call for transparency and accountability echoes the sentiment of educators globally, serving as a moral compass and guiding our choices around technology in the classroom. As we reflect on how we can harness AI to create a human-centered education, it's imperative to realize the breadth and importance of this conversation about AI tools in education and other industries. Much of the world is now paying attention and weighing in on how to regulate generative AI tools, from innovating industry to increasing personal influence and wealth.

Embarking on the road to AI in education, teachers encounter four critical speed bumps:

- **Privacy and Data Security**, requiring vigilance in handling student information
- **Bias and Fairness**, demanding awareness and intervention to ensure equitable learning
- **Transparency**, fostering trust through clear understanding and communication
- **Accountability**, establishing responsibility in the use and outcomes of AI tools

Navigating these speed bumps is essential for a safe, ethical, and effective journey into the world of AI-enhanced teaching and learning.

Is There an Ethics and Regulations Guide for Teachers?

There are different ways to create ethics and regulations for teachers using AI. This is my version of how to do this work.

As we stand at the edge of a digital revolution in education, the promise of AI tools in classrooms is both thrilling and daunting. It's exciting to imagine our students benefiting from the individualized attention and the innovative learning techniques that AI tools provide.

Yet, we are equally aware of the need for caution as we tread this new path. Stepping into the AI-filled classroom journey requires a blend of enthusiasm and skepticism. As educators, we have a unique role to play, embracing the transformative potential of AI while ensuring we safeguard the interests of our most important responsibility for society—our students.

An informed teacher is a powerful teacher.

So, how do we navigate this journey responsibly? *AI Goes to School* is a roadmap for the conscientious educator ready to harness AI's potential while also navigating the winding road of ethical challenges.

What Does an Ethical AI Classroom Look Like?

As we think critically about using AI tools like ChatGPT, Google Gemini, and Microsoft Copilot, and we embark on our journey into the expanding world of AI, let's delve into the ethical conundrums that these generative AI tools introduce in our classrooms.

Picture, if you will, Mrs. Baker, a veteran math teacher, as she embarks on her first steps into the world of AI with all the enthusiasm of a child in a candy store. She was excited about the possibilities these shiny new tools offer. But like any novelty, AI comes with challenges as well as benefits.

Beginning her journey, Mrs. Baker enthusiastically threw open the doors to AI in her classroom. But she soon realized that she needed more than just enthusiasm. She needed understanding. She needed vigilance. She needed transparency. And she needed to establish clear lines of accountability. Thus, she set off on her quest for ethical AI use.

The first ethical speed bump that Mrs. Baker encountered was a considerable one: **Privacy and Data Security**. She learned that each time she used an AI tool, it greedily devoured data, munching on everything from student names to performance statistics. While this feast of information aided the AI in delivering personalized learning experiences, it also raised concerns about who was watching the watchers. So, she decided to focus much of her AI use on teacher-centered tools to make sure she observed student privacy policies and laws.

To navigate this concern before she began, Mrs. Baker cleared her use of the chosen AI tool by reaching out to her building administrator and IT department. She clarified school and district policies and ensured she was on the right side of data privacy laws, such as AB-2799 in California or the Student Online Personal Protection Act in Illinois. Next, she communicated transparently with parents about the nature of data collection, securing their informed consent when necessary. But her vigilance didn't end at adoption— she remained attentive to any updates or changes in the tool's data practices so she would continue adhering to privacy standards.

Just when Mrs. Baker thought she had navigated the choppy waters of Data Security, she found herself in the eye of another storm: **Bias and Fairness.** The AI tools, she realized, were nothing more than mirrors reflecting the data they were trained on. If the data carried a bias, the AI would unwittingly become a mouthpiece for it. She saw how this bias could twist the learning experience, offering skewed content and unfair assessments. Not one to back down, Mrs. Baker equipped herself to recognize and mitigate such biases, standing as a bastion against unfairness.

To truly understand AI in education, she dove deep into their workings, learning their decision-making processes and student data use. She learned about the AI tools' efforts to ensure fairness and combat bias. She sought out AI that respected data privacy laws and had robust data security measures in place. She kept a watchful eye for any signs of bias and stepped in to course-correct whenever she spotted them.

The next ethical conundrum lurking around the corner was the shadowy figure of **Transparency.** Without understanding how AI processed data and made decisions, Mrs. Baker felt like she was driving blind. So, she armed herself by searching for ways to use the AI tools transparently, which included sharing when and how she would use them. Transparency, she realized, was not just about understanding the tools but also building trust with her students and their parents.

To promote transparency, she initiated open discussions about AI in the classroom with her students and their parents. Mrs. Baker shared the benefits and potential pitfalls of using these tools, sparking conversations and instilling trust. She sought out professional development opportunities, attending training sessions on specific AI tools and seminars on the ethical implications of AI.

Finally, Mrs. Baker came face-to-face with the daunting specter of **Accountability.** As AI tools became an integral part of her classroom, she pondered who would be held responsible if issues arose. This brought to light the importance of setting clear accountability structures that outlined who would be responsible if an AI tool faltered or misbehaved. In addition, she grappled with the ideas of plagiarism, academic integrity for when to use AI tools, citation protocols when she or her students consulted and used AI tools, and other important implications to make sure they were all using AI tools thoughtfully, critically, and responsibly.

At the end of the unit, as Mrs. Baker closed her classroom door and reflected on her journey with AI, she knew she had taken the right steps. She ensured that the integration of AI into her classroom was not just effective but also ethical. In doing so, she created a learning environment that respected and protected the rights of all her students.

AI holds the promise of a brighter future for education. As we move forward, we must navigate the ethical speed bumps wisely, just like Mrs. Baker. Let's embrace the exciting potential of AI while also safeguarding the rights and well-being of our students.

MAKING LITERACY THE FIRST STEP

The first phase of our expedition into AI is to understand it. What is AI? How does it work? What are the potential uses and benefits in education? And equally important, what are the ethical considerations it brings to the fore? The answers to these questions form the foundation of our AI literacy. *AI Goes to School* is your starting point, providing you with the basics of AI and its role in the educational sphere.

But don't stop here. Augment your newfound knowledge by seeking out professional development opportunities in AI. Participate in related workshops or online courses, join professional networks, and engage with scholarly and industry research on AI in education. Why? Because an informed teacher is a powerful teacher. You will not only be equipped to use AI tools ethically and effectively but will also be in a position to foster critical awareness and digital literacy among your students.

NAVIGATING THE DATA PRIVACY MAZE

As we make our way further into the digital world of AI in education, we must navigate the complex maze of student data privacy. The days of file cabinets with locks and sealed envelopes storing student information have given way to databases and cloud storage. In this era of rapid digitization, managing student information has taken on a demanding level of complexity. When tech-savvy meets tech-risky, you're the gatekeeper.

With ever-changing data privacy laws emerging in many regions, staying ahead of the curve is our responsibility as educators. Fortunately, schools are rising to this challenge, investing heavily in training sessions to keep us updated and informed.

The next stage of our journey takes us through the challenging terrain of privacy laws, such as the Family Educational Rights and Privacy Act (FERPA) in the US and the General Data Protection Regulation (GDPR) in Europe. These regulations are the stars guiding our journey, setting boundaries on how we can use, protect, and share sensitive student data. By becoming well-versed in these laws, we make informed choices about AI tools and prioritize our students' privacy. As educators, we are the vanguard of ethical AI use. Staying up-to-date with data privacy laws, as challenging as it may seem, is an essential part of our journey. With knowledge and an advocacy spirit, we can responsibly choose and implement technology tools in our classrooms.

Federal US and European Union Student Privacy Laws

In the US, FERPA is the primary law protecting student privacy by limiting who can access student records and how. It also says why these people or entities can access records and what they have to do to keep the information safe. Other laws like PPRA also make sure students' personal information stays private in surveys, studies, or reports that get federal funding. Schools that receive funding for special education must keep students' personal details confidential.

Not only the federal government but forty-two states and Washington, DC, have put more than 128 extra student privacy laws on the books (Stone, 2022). Schools must make a concerted effort to follow all the rules and train teachers on best practices.

The most important objective is that these laws shield students' sensitive data. Schools adopting AI and other edtech tools must ensure students' information stays protected and private. Your most important directive is to only use tools that meet all legal requirements for responsible data use.

While privacy laws can be complicated, they exist to give students and their parents and guardians more control and transparency over their personal information. With AI potentially expanding data collection, it's crucial that schools operate ethically and keep students' well-being in mind. It bears repeating: Teachers play a key role in advocating for students' privacy rights and using technology in a way that respects those rights.

UNITED STATES FEDERAL LAWS

Table 3.1 is a summary of the relevant US federal laws that impact student data privacy as of the printing of this book.

Law	Summary
Family Educational Rights and Privacy Act (FERPA)	Safeguards student privacy by limiting who may access student records, specifying for what purpose they may access those records, and detailing what rules they have to follow when accessing them.
Protection of Pupil Rights Amendment (PPRA)	Outlines restrictions pertaining to student privacy in federally funded surveys or evaluations.
Children's Online Privacy Protection Act (COPPA)	Requires websites and online services to obtain parental consent before collecting personal information from children under age thirteen.

Table 3.1: US Federal Student Privacy Laws.

EUROPEAN UNION LAWS

Table 3.2 is a quick summary of current and proposed privacy laws in the European Union.

Law	Summary
General Data Protection Regulation (GDPR)	A European privacy law that became the new legal backbone on data protection and privacy in the EU in May 2018. It covers many areas of the digital sphere, and it was applied to every member state within the EU.
Proposed EU AI Act	The European Union's AI Act is the first major act to regulate AI. The legislation includes provisions for student data privacy. The act passed the European Parliament on March 13, 2024.

Table 3.2: EU Privacy Laws.

UNITED STATES INDIVIDUAL STATE LAWS

Many states have recently passed new laws to strengthen the protection of K–12 students' sensitive data. Since 2013 when inBloom Inc. privacy concerns first arose, at least forty states have placed additional student privacy laws on the books. Simply said (but not simply done), schools need to understand all the laws that apply to them and make sure they follow the rules.

School and district administrators, as well as classroom teachers, need to:

1. Understand the laws in their state and region to protect student privacy proactively.
2. Establish clear policies and review processes for new technologies to ensure service providers also respect students' privacy rights.
3. Stay up-to-date on laws and advocate for strong privacy protections.

Key state laws include:*

- **California:** Mandates that schools protect all K–12 student personal information. Passed the Student Online Personal Protection Act (SOPPA) to safeguard student data collected by education technology.
- **Colorado:** Requires schools to publish a list of the student data currently collected and stored by the state's education department.
- **Connecticut:** Requires schools to notify parents annually in writing about student data privacy and security policies.
- **Illinois:** Mandates that schools protect all K–12 student data. Passed the Student Online Personal Protection Act (SOPPA) to safeguard student data collected by education technology.
- **Minnesota and Montana:** Requires schools to get parental permission before sharing student data with third-party service providers.
- **New York:** Mandates that schools inform parents of their rights to protect children's personal information under state and federal law.
- **Tennessee:** Regulates student data collection and use to protect privacy in K–12 and early education. Schools must follow additional rules for pre-K and early intervention programs.

In the following scenarios, teachers act as guardians of their students' data privacy while leveraging the power of AI in their classrooms. By understanding

---

* If you are looking for your state's privacy laws, visit micahminer.com for a list of helpful links to these sites.

the legal landscape and making thoughtful and informed choices about AI tools, they exemplify how teachers can navigate the intricate dance of AI and ethics in their classrooms.

Scenario 1

THE CASE OF UNINTENDED DATA SHARING (CALIFORNIA'S DATA PRIVACY LAWS)

In sunny California, fifth-grade teacher Mrs. Gonzales is using an AI-powered learning chatbot that teachers can use to enhance her students' learning. She believes in the system's personalized learning paths that offer customized educational content to each student with teacher oversight. However, as she navigates this high-tech tool, she also needs to consider the ethical implications tied to her students' privacy.

Given that the AI system collects a plethora of personal data from her students, the six California state laws come into play. These laws extend student privacy protections to student personal data, ensuring that even the youngest learners are safeguarded. Further, these ensure the protection of student data collected by educational technology.

Solution:
The ethical considerations here are manifold. First, Mrs. Gonzales needs to ensure that the AI tool complies with these laws. This entails checking if the tool has safeguards in place to protect students' data from unauthorized access—a potential breach that could have grave consequences.

Second, she must establish that she's using the data solely for the intended educational purpose and it isn't being shared without consent, sold, or used for targeted advertising, all of which would violate the principles laid out in these important student data privacy regulations. Transparency regarding data practices, a primary tenet of ethical AI use, is pivotal here.

To ensure she's using AI ethically, Mrs. Gonzales asks for the AI provider's data handling and privacy policies to see that they're aligned with California student data privacy laws. Also, regular communication with parents about the AI tools being used, the data collected, and the measures in place to protect this data fosters trust as well as adherence to these privacy laws.

Scenario 2

THE TRANSPARENCY IMPERATIVE
(ILLINOIS'S SOPPA)

Moving to the East, Illinois high school science teacher Mr. Richards employs an AI tool that provides immersive virtual reality experiences to help his students grasp complex scientific concepts. However, the tool's data tracking features pose a myriad of ethical considerations that Mr. Richards must address.

Illinois's SOPPA mandates that schools provide parents with a list of online services and applications their children will be using in school and information about how their children's data will be used and protected. Additionally, the law requires districts to provide parents with annual written notification of their data privacy and security policies.

Solution:
Mr. Richards's ethical considerations involve ensuring the AI tool's practices align with these laws. He must be transparent about how the AI tool uses the students' data, whether it is essential for the learning experience, and whether the data is securely stored and deleted when no longer needed.

To ethically employ this AI tool, Mr. Richards engages in regular communication with students and their parents, elucidating the AI tool's data practices and how they adhere to SOPPA. Transparency about the school's data privacy and security policies in line with the SOPPA law can further bolster the ethical deployment of this AI tool.

Scenario 3

PRIORITIZING CONSENT
(MINNEAPOLIS'S STUDENT DATA PRIVACY LAW)

Over in Minneapolis, Mr. Benson, a middle school history teacher, has found an interactive AI-based app that makes learning historical events engaging and interactive. However, Minneapolis law mandates that schools obtain parental consent before sharing student data with third-party service providers.

Solution:

Mr. Benson must establish that the AI tool isn't just beneficial educationally but also respects privacy requirements. As such, before he rolls out the app in his classroom, he seeks parental consent for their children to use the application, explicitly explaining what data the AI tool will collect and how it will be used and protected.

To ensure ethical use, Mr. Benson conducts an open house to introduce the AI tool to the parents and obtain their written consent. Regular updates about any changes in the tool's data collection practices further build trust and provide compliance with the law.

Scenario 4

ENFORCING PROTECTION
(NEW YORK'S STUDENT DATA PRIVACY LAW)

In bustling New York City, a middle school English teacher, Ms. Rodriguez, employs an AI-powered tool that uses students' writing samples to provide personalized feedback and improvement suggestions. The tool could be a game-changer for her students, but New York law stipulates that schools must notify parents about their rights under federal and state law to protect their children's personal information.

Ms. Rodriguez's ethical considerations involve ensuring that the AI tool maintains the confidentiality of student data and doesn't inadvertently expose any sensitive information. Additionally, she must make sure the tool doesn't store any data longer than necessary, adhering to data minimization principles.

Solution:

To guarantee ethical use, she provides a detailed guide to parents, outlining their rights concerning their children's data and how the AI tool respects these rights. She promptly communicates any changes to the tool's data practices and keeps an open line of communication for parents to voice any concerns or queries. To respect this, she made sure that the parents signed off on the use of the tool in addition to clearing it with school administration and the IT department.

Scenario 5

ADHERENCE TO LEGISLATION
(TENNESSEE'S DATA PRIVACY LAWS)

Down in Tennessee, Mr. Palmer, a high school math teacher, uses an AI-enabled tool that offers adaptive learning experiences based on student performance. However, Tennessee's privacy laws protect K–12 students by regulating the creation of student data at school and how that data may be used and shared.

Mr. Palmer must ensure that the AI tool abides by these regulations, safeguarding student data from inappropriate use. The tool must only use student data for the intended educational purposes and must not share it without the required permissions.

Solution:

To provide ethical use, Mr. Palmer checks the tool's compliance with Tennessee laws before introducing it in his class. He keeps parents informed about the tool's use, the kind of data it collects, and the measures in place to protect this data, demonstrating his commitment to protecting his students' privacy.

In each scenario, the teachers are mindful and proactive to ensure ethical AI use in their classrooms. They accomplish this by adhering to their respective state privacy laws, maintaining transparency about the AI tools' data practices, and keeping an open channel of communication with parents.

How Do I Know if I'm Using AI Ethically?

As the drumbeat of the march of AI into our classrooms grows louder, teachers find themselves facing the thrilling yet daunting task of harnessing its potential in an ethical manner. Taking the reins of this transformative technology, educators must keep their students' best interests as their guiding North Star.

Teachers need to dive headfirst into understanding AI, the framework within which it operates, and its multifaceted implications. Immerse yourself in the world of AI, taking on the role of lifelong learner as you navigate professional development programs, seminars, and workshops that demystify this technology. Staying current with research and best practices helps you wield the power of AI responsibly while minimizing any unintended fallout.

> You help shape a future where AI is a boon to education, a future where technology amplifies the humanity in education rather than overshadows it.

Navigating the labyrinth of data privacy laws and regulations is a fundamental requisite in this journey. Grasping the nuances of legal acts such as FERPA or GDPR equips educators with the knowledge they need to ensure that AI tools comply with the law, thereby safeguarding their students' personal information.

Remember, privacy policies alone don't protect students' rights or build trust—those are realized through the judgments and actions of the educators using the technology ... and that's where our LEAP framework from Chapter 1 comes in again as a guide to implementing AI in the classroom. Here's a quick review:

- **Learner-Centered:** The focus should always be on our students.
- **Ethical Adoption:** Remain alert to issues of equity, inclusion, and data privacy.
- **Adaptive Personalization:** Chatbot suggestions are meant to inform our decisions, not make them for us.
- **Performance Reflection:** Continuously evaluate the impact of these tools on learning, experience, privacy, and equity.

The mission is clear: We must safeguard our students' privacy, guarantee fairness, foster transparency, and maintain the irreplaceable human touch that lies at the heart of teaching. By taking these steps, you help shape a future where AI is a boon to education, a future where technology amplifies the humanity in education rather than overshadows it.

To this end, here are some pivotal steps that educators can follow:

SEEKING DIVERSE PERSPECTIVES

When deciding how to use AI in the classroom, seek input from people with different viewpoints. The kaleidoscope of diverse perspectives from students, parents, colleagues, and community members sheds invaluable light on potential ethical concerns and solutions. By actively seeking and incorporating this information, teachers establish a climate where AI respects the diversity of the classroom and champions inclusion and equity.

Promoting equity and empowering all students through AI requires acknowledging diversity in abilities, backgrounds, values, and learning needs. While one approach may inspire some students, it may discourage or disadvantage others if not designed thoughtfully with all learners in mind.

Diverse perspectives reveal different experiences, concerns, and impacts that teachers alone may not see. Students and parents provide direct feedback on what AI tools and data use they feel most comfortable with. Colleagues may have alternative insights or spot consequences that aren't immediately apparent. Community stakeholders represent the interests of various student groups.

Considering all views helps to address potential inequities or harm, especially for marginalized students, that can arise from technology misuse or oversight. What seems a positive, convenient use of AI for some students may present challenges or compromise privacy and access for others. With broad, inclusive discussions, schools can choose tools and set policies responsive to every student's needs.

PRACTICING CONTINUOUS REFLECTION

Ethical AI use is not a one-time setup but a continuous process of reflection and refinement. Regularly assess the impacts of the AI tools you're using, gather feedback from students, and look for signs of issues such as data breaches or bias in AI outputs. If problems arise, be ready to reassess your use of the tool in question and, if necessary, seek out alternatives.

The next vital step is to teach your students to become literate about AI. Explain to them how AI works, what it's used for, and why we must consider ethics. Give students the knowledge they need to thoughtfully navigate a world filled with AI. By promoting AI literacy, teachers empower students to approach new technologies with an informed, socially conscious mindset.

INCORPORATING ACCEPTABLE USE POLICIES AND GUIDELINES

The conversation around a school's acceptable use policies, academic integrity, and guidelines should include AI tools in general and chatbots specifically. Discuss answers to these questions:

- What are your assumptions and practices as teachers and administrators concerning these topics?
- What kind of content should be taught in a twenty-first-century curriculum when AI tools can provide so much information?
- How does a human-centered education that promotes critical thinking and ethics incorporate AI tools to enhance and augment learning not become the center of education?

Generative AI tools like ChatGPT, Google Gemini, Anthropic's Claude, and Microsoft Copilot, as well as others, have the capabilities to generate high-quality content. While they can be valuable learning aids for students, there's also a risk that these tools could be used inappropriately to generate complete assignments, bypassing the learning process altogether. We must establish clear guidelines around the use of AI tools for schoolwork. AI can be used as a brainstorming tool or inspiration, but the final work should always be the student's creation. It's imperative that teachers teach academic integrity in this AI era and are able to identify AI-generated work.

Including AI ethics and operations in a classroom curriculum equips students to use AI responsibly. Overall, policies for ethical AI require an inclusive, iterative approach ... one that keeps human development at the center. AI allows us to enhance creativity and critical thinking. Here is a basic guideline that school administrators and teachers can consider when developing policies around the use of AI-generative tools. There are three main areas:

1. Academic Integrity Policy
2. Acceptable Use Policy (AUP)
3. AI Literacy Program

Keep in mind that this is a starting point, and individual institutions can tailor these suggestions to fit their specific needs and context.

1. Academic Integrity Policy:

It's vital that schools revisit the topics of learning in this age of technology. When students use AI tools, they still need to create original work, understand materials, and defend responses. AI may provide information or suggestions to enhance creativity and critical thinking but may not be used to bypass the learning process.

We must also reconsider our assumptions concerning plagiarism and cheating in light of AI and redefine the boundaries of what constitutes academic dishonesty. Traditionally, copying from a textbook or another student was deemed as plagiarism, but now—when a student uses AI to generate a paragraph, an essay, or even a poem—what does this mean in terms of originality and authenticity? Check out Chapter 6 for more on this subject.

Step 1: Create an academic integrity policy to clearly define what constitutes plagiarism and cheating in the context of AI, providing examples and guidelines. Table 3.3 offers a few samples:

Element	Description
Definition of AI-Generated Plagiarism	A clear definition of what constitutes plagiarism when using AI tools (ex: directly using a paragraph generated by AI without adding any personal input or insight can be considered plagiarism).
Use of AI for Brainstorming	Guidelines on using AI as a tool for brainstorming or structuring thoughts (ex: students can use AI to help with ideas, but the final work should be their own).
Referencing AI Output	Guidelines on how to cite or reference AI output. Students must cite the AI tool used in their work just like with a human author.
Detection Tools and Consequences	Explanation of the detection methods used to identify AI-generated content. Explanation of the consequences for violations.

Table 3.3: Example of an Academic Integrity Policy.

Step 2: Share your school's academic integrity policy with your students, their parents, and community stakeholders.

Here's an example of this policy in student-friendly language:

What is AI-generated plagiarism?

AI-generated plagiarism is when you use an AI tool like ChatGPT to write something for you and then submit it as your own work without saying where it came from. This includes copying and pasting text from the AI or modifying text from the AI without citing it.

Can I use AI to help me?
Yes, you can use AI tools to help you come up with ideas or plan out your work. But the final work you submit needs to be written in your own words. Think of AI as giving you suggestions, not doing the work for you.

How do I give credit to AI?
If you use something from an AI tool in your work, you need to say where it came from, just like you would with information from a website or book. Make sure to mention the name of the AI tool.

What if I break the rules?
If we find you submitted work created by AI without citing it, there will be instructive consequences such as failing grades.

The key points are:
1. Don't submit AI-generated work as your own without citing it.
2. Use AI for help and ideas, but do your own work.
3. Always cite AI sources.
4. There are instructive consequences for violations of this policy.

2. Acceptable Use Policy (AUP)

It's important to establish this policy to maximize the promise of AI as a tool for learning while mitigating risks. The key lies in an approach that is human-centered, inclusive, and committed to open dialogue. We must start by defining ethical AI use in education by using AI transparently and ethically to support human decision-making, not replace it. It requires safeguarding privacy, security, and fairness and avoiding bias or an overreliance on technology.

Step 1: This policy should provide clear guidelines on acceptable and unacceptable uses of AI tools. Table 3.4 shares an example.

Element	Description
Acceptable Use	Outline acceptable ways to use AI tools in the learning process (e.g., generating ideas, structuring arguments, correcting grammar).
Unacceptable Use	Define uses that are not allowed (e.g., generating entire assignments or papers using AI).
Data Privacy	Explain how AI tools should be used in a way that respects data privacy (e.g., avoid inputting personal or sensitive information into AI tools).
Safety and Respect	Guidelines on how to use AI tools safely and respectfully without causing harm or offense.

Table 3.4: Example of an Acceptable Use Policy.

Step 2: Here's an example of a student-friendly AUP statement based on this rubric. Remember to modify this for your location and educational context.

How to Use AI Tools the Right Way
AI tools can help you learn! Here are good ways to use them:
- Come up with ideas for projects
- Plan out essays or papers
- Fix grammar and spelling
- Translate languages
- Summarize difficult texts
- Write code

But don't let AI do all the work for you. You need to add your own thoughts and effort.

Here's Stuff You Should Not Do:
- Turn in assignments that an AI tool fully wrote for you
- Copy other people's work using AI
- Create harmful, fake, or mean content with AI
- Use AI in illegal or unethical ways

Keep Your Info Safe

Be careful what information you put into AI tools. Avoid sharing private stuff like:

- Your name, address, or phone number
- Financial information
- Medical information
- School records and grades

When in doubt, don't put personal info into AI!

Use AI Respectfully

Don't create anything with AI that could hurt others or make people upset. Avoid content that is:

- Violent
- Hateful
- Biased against groups
- Sexual or inappropriate
- False
- Damaging to someone's reputation

Check Your Work

AI tools are still learning.

- Review and vet AI content every time.
- Never turn anything in without double-checking the information.
- Always edit and fix mistakes.

Cite Your Sources

- If you use AI as a source, cite it like you would a website or book.

Follow these rules to use AI responsibly!

3. AI Literacy Program

Learning and teaching how AI works and how to use it responsibly is essential. Students, teachers, and parents should understand AI's role as an educational tool, not as a shortcut. An open dialogue with all stakeholders helps address challenges and explore opportunities (like the lack of teacher AI skills or data privacy concerns). We learn from collective experiences.

Step 1: Create a structured program to teach students about AI, its capabilities, and ethical considerations. Table 3.5 shares some AI literacy topics.

Element	Description
Understanding AI	Lessons on what AI is, how it works, and its capabilities and limitations.
Ethical Considerations	Lessons on ethical considerations around AI, including data privacy, bias, transparency, and fairness.
Using AI Responsibly	Lessons on how to use AI tools responsibly, effectively, and ethically in academic work.
Future of AI	Lessons on the future of AI and how it's likely to shape various fields, including education.

Table 3.5: Example of an AI Literacy Program.

Here is one example of how an AI Literacy Program could be structured based on this information.

AI Literacy Program:
Empowering Ethical and Informed AI Users

Introduction

This AI Literacy Program provides students with a comprehensive understanding of artificial intelligence and its ethical implications, responsible use, and future impact. It is divided into four main modules, each addressing a critical aspect of AI.

Module 1: Understanding AI

Objective

Equip students with foundational knowledge about what AI is, how it functions, and its capabilities and limitations.

Lesson Plans

1. What Is AI?—Introduction to AI, its history, and types of AI (Narrow AI and General AI).

2. How Does AI Work?—Basics of machine learning, neural networks, and Natural Language Processing.
3. What Are Its Capabilities and Limitations?—Case studies showcasing what AI can and cannot do.

Module 2: Ethical Considerations

Objective
Introduce students to the ethical dimensions of AI, focusing on data privacy, bias, transparency, and fairness.

Lesson Plans
1. Data Privacy—The importance of data privacy, how AI uses data, and best practices for safeguarding information.
2. Bias in AI—How bias creeps into AI algorithms and how to mitigate it.
3. Transparency and Fairness—The need for transparent AI algorithms and equitable access to AI technologies.

Module 3: Using AI Responsibly

Objective
Teach students how to use AI tools responsibly, effectively, and ethically in academic work.

Lesson Plans
1. AI for Research and Learning—Guidelines for using AI for research, generating ideas, and learning enhancement.
2. Academic Integrity—Rules around citing AI-generated content and avoiding plagiarism.
3. Responsible Interaction—How to interact respectfully and responsibly with AI, focusing on chatbots and AI teaching assistants.

Module 4: The Future of AI

Objective
Explore how AI is likely to evolve and its potential impact on various fields, including education.

Lesson Plans
1. AI in Future Classrooms—Speculations about how AI could transform educational settings in the future.

2. AI in the Job Market—Discussion on the types of jobs that AI could create and render obsolete.

3. AI and Society—An overview of how AI could influence societal norms, ethics, and daily life.

Conclusion

This program concludes with a capstone project where students demonstrate what they learned through a speech for their administration, district leaders, board of education, or community. They share and apply what they've learned about AI and how they will use it ethically in their studies and their careers. This serves as a comprehensive reflection of their understanding and thoughts on the responsible use of AI in education and beyond.

Here's a short story to illustrate these policy ideas and topics.

The Symphony of Bytes and Books

In the sunny suburbs of Silicon Valley, nestled amid tech giants, was a small school named Quantum Valley High School. The school's librarian, Mr. Carlos, was known for his love of stories, encyclopedic knowledge, and now his innovative use of AI in the library.

One day, Mr. Carlos introduced a new AI tool powered by ChatGPT to the students visiting the library. He explained that the AI assistant could help with homework, generate creative story ideas, and even answer trivia questions. However, he was clear about the rules.

"This is not a shortcut to your assignments or an opportunity to misuse technology," he warned, referring to the Academic Integrity Policy. He explained that using the AI tool to complete entire assignments was unethical and akin to plagiarism. However, using it as a study aid, a brainstorming tool, or a writing companion was completely fine.

Lucas, an aspiring writer, found the tool particularly helpful. He would start a story and then let the AI tool continue it, learning how to build exciting plots and create dynamic characters. While the tool often gave interesting ideas, Lucas was always the master of his stories, tailoring the AI's suggestions to fit his unique voice and vision.

In contrast, Jake, another student, attempted to pass off an AI-generated essay as his own work. Mr. Carlos, having integrated an AI plagiarism detection tool, recognized the AI-generated text and took the opportunity to reinforce the school's Academic Integrity Policy. Jake learned an important lesson about the difference between using AI as a tool for learning versus as a way to avoid work.

Mr. Carlos also emphasized the Acceptable Use Policy. He reminded the students never to share personal information with the AI. As an exercise in understanding privacy implications, he even held a workshop demonstrating how information shared online could be misused.

Additionally, the students were taught to treat the AI tool with respect, ensuring their interactions were polite and constructive. Mr. Carlos explained that this was good practice for their future interactions in a digitally dominated world.

Mr. Carlos also introduced a series of "Understanding AI" workshops. Students learned how AI worked, its capabilities, its limitations, and the ethical implications of AI technology. They were encouraged to critically engage with the tool, understanding its strengths and shortcomings.

Over time, the Quantum Valley High School library became more than a place to find books. It was a hub of innovative AI use ... a model for other schools. Students learned to operate AI ethically and effectively, enhancing their learning while maintaining their academic integrity. The symphony of bytes and books played harmoniously in the school, creating an environment rich in learning and exploration.

This story showcases how AI can be integrated and managed in a school library setting, emphasizing the policies and principles for ethical usage. It offers another perspective on how teachers can reinforce academic integrity and acceptable use while also enhancing learning with AI.

The narrative of Quantum Valley High School's journey with AI fits seamlessly into the LEAP framework, illustrating its principles in action.

Learner-Centered: Just like Lucas in our story, students remain at the core of AI adoption, using a ChatGPT-based AI tool as support for their creative endeavors and homework rather than a substitute for their own efforts. Mr. Carlos's emphasis on students being the "masters of their stories" aligns perfectly with this concept.

Ethical Adoption: The incident with Jake learning about academic integrity through Mr. Carlos's application of the Acceptable Use Policy reflects the commitment to ethical adoption. The students are taught not just how to use the AI tool but also how to use it responsibly, ensuring equity, inclusion, and privacy.

Adaptive Personalization: Lucas's creative writing journey with ChatGPT showcases adaptive personalization. The AI tool developed from his narrative, offering suggestions that Lucas then molded to fit his unique voice and vision. It served as a guide, assisting Lucas, but it was Lucas who made the final decisions.

Performance Reflection: Regular evaluation is evident in Mr. Carlos's vigilance and the use of an AI plagiarism detection tool to catch instances of misuse. He also regularly evaluates students' understanding of AI and its capabilities and limitations through the "Understanding AI" workshops.

By ensuring that AI adoption was learner-centered, ethically adopted, adaptively personalized, and performance-reflective, Quantum Valley High School successfully navigated the challenges of integrating AI into its educational system. (Check out micahminer.com for rubric examples to evaluate students' use of AI tools.)

REBOOT

So, let's wrap up this long (but hopefully helpful) chapter ...

In the rapidly evolving landscape of education, AI integration has profound implications. As we embrace these powerful tools, it becomes more crucial than ever to uphold our commitment to ethical use, academic integrity, and AI literacy. These principles provide the guiding light, illuminating our path as we navigate the exciting yet intricate intersection of education and AI.

Acceptable Use Policies (AUPs) form the backbone of our ethical approach, ensuring a respectful and responsible environment for AI interactions. They not only delineate the boundaries of appropriate behavior but also serve to protect students, teachers, and institutions from potential harm. As educators, we must ensure that these policies explicitly address principles like privacy, data security, and bias avoidance. AUPs should be ingrained into the daily fabric of our classrooms through consistent reinforcement and open discussion.

However, the stewardship of ethical AI use does not end with AUPs. Academic integrity remains at the core of educational ethics, preserving the sanctity of learning. With AI, academic integrity takes on a nuanced dimension: using AI as a tool for enhancement and inspiration, not a shortcut to circumvent personal effort.

Also, to truly empower our students and educators in this AI-integration journey, an AI literacy program is indispensable. By gaining a solid understanding of AI's capabilities, limitations, and ethical considerations, we cultivate a community that harnesses the potential of AI while remaining mindful of its pitfalls.

Our vision should not be merely to adopt AI but to weave it organically into our educational practices, always with respect, integrity, and understanding as we focus on harnessing the tools for a human-centered education.

For more information, read the US Department of Education's May 2023 update on AI in education entitled *Artificial Intelligence and the Future of Teaching and Learning: Insights and Recommendations*. Let's go over some highlights from the report:

Key Insights from the Report

1. AI enables new ways for students and teachers to interact using speech, gestures, drawings, and more. AI can generate human-like responses to support students with disabilities.
2. AI addresses differences in how students learn. AI tools adapt to students' diverse learning needs, language skills, abilities, and more. They provide step-by-step support, not just correct/incorrect feedback.
3. AI powerfully adapts to how students learn as it happens, not just to their answers. These adaptations help students progress by using their strengths and overcoming obstacles.
4. AI improves and increases the quality and quantity of feedback for students and teachers. It suggests resources to improve teaching and learning.
5. Educators help design AI tools to enhance their work and better engage/support students.
6. We want technology to complement humans, not replace them. Like electric bikes, not robot vacuums. Humans stay fully in control and aware, but AI lightens the burdens and boosts efforts.

Calls to Action –
The Path Forward for AI in Education

1. **Keep Humans in the Loop:** We must reject the misconception of AI replacing teachers. The human touch in education is irreplaceable, and AI should serve as a tool to enhance human capabilities, not replace them.
2. **Align AI with Our Vision for Education:** AI tools must fit into our shared vision for teaching and learning, evaluated not just on outcomes but also on how well they integrate into our educational philosophies.

3. **Design with Modern Learning Principles in Mind:** AI systems should be designed with a strong understanding of modern learning principles and the wisdom of educational practitioners. They should be culturally responsive, fair, and inclusive, especially for students with disabilities and English learners.

4. **Build Trust in Technology:** We must strive to create trust in AI-enabled educational technologies, understanding that it's a two-way street. This trust grows as educators, innovators, researchers, and policymakers work together toward this goal.

5. **Educate the Educators:** A key to the successful integration of AI in education is to keep educators informed and involved at each step. They must be prepared to explore AI's potential and understand its risks.

6. **Focus AI Research and Development on Context and Trust:** AI research should focus on understanding how AI adapts to different learning contexts and enhances trust and safety in AI-enabled education systems.

7. **Craft Education-Specific Guidelines:** With AI's unique capabilities come unique risks. Hence, it's necessary to develop specific guidelines and guardrails for AI in education with inputs from all stakeholders.

So ... let's gear up to explore AI in education, enhancing learning experiences with the power of AI and ensuring a safe, inclusive, and exciting journey ahead for all our learners!

Part II
Integrating AI in Your Teaching

If students get a sound education in the history, social effects, and psychological biases of technology, they may grow to be adults who use technology rather than be used by it.

— Neil Postman, author, media theorist, and cultural critic

Image P2: Classroom assistants—bridging traditional learning with AI innovations.

Chapter 4
Using AI-Assisted Lesson Planning and Content Generation

By far, the greatest danger of artificial intelligence is that people conclude too early that they understand it.

— Eliezer Yudkowsky, computer scientist and AI pioneer

Image 4.1: Where bytes meet books—AI assists educators to streamline lesson planning.

W elcome, fellow educator, to a brave new world of teaching and learning! A realm where technology and pedagogy unite, where AI becomes less robot and more collaborator. For too long, we've struggled alone, planning lessons into the wee hours and tirelessly hunting for that perfect activity. Well, friends, our days of isolation are over. The age of AI is here, and with it a promise: empowered educators, engaged students, and an educational landscape tailored to every learner's needs.

But first, a reality check. Artificial intelligence is not a magic bullet. Its true power emerges only when guided by us—the shepherds of knowledge and guardians of our society's futures. We set the learning goals. We spark the flame of curiosity. And we impart the empathy no algorithm can replicate. So, think of AI as your lesson-planning sidekick, suggesting activities and discussion prompts tailored to your students. You add your spice, modify the recipe, and voilà! You have a lesson plan that's both cutting edge and classroom-ready.

Of course, vigilance is key. We must ensure this technology uplifts, not diminishes, our humanity. Used judiciously, though, AI frees us from the late nights of trying to create lessons that help reteach content from your learning goals that you're surprised to find your students didn't understand. Need to meet the lesson plan deadline for school administration? Let our AI thought partner and collaborator assist. We then reinvest that energy into building stronger relationships with our students, who blossom best when tended by present, energized educators. AI-assisted planning gives us back those precious hours to inspire young minds.

Beyond the present possibilities, we must also envision the future horizons of educational AI. Imagine intelligent agents adapting lessons to each student's emotions, creating psychologically responsive learning. Or ethically customized AI toolkits, mitigating risks from the start. The classroom of tomorrow awaits our vision, so let's dream big!

How Can AI Help Me in the Classroom?

As we journey into the realm of AI-assisted education, it's essential to first unpack the concept of an AI sidekick. In essence, AI-assisted lesson planning is about employing AI tools to design, adjust, and enrich your curricula. AI tailors lessons based on individual student needs, enhancing personalization and streamlining lesson creation and freeing up valuable time for educators. Similarly, AI-assisted content generation can produce or modify educational content such as quizzes and interactive assignments.

The potential of AI in education is vast, yet it's not a panacea. AI's strength lies in providing personalized, scalable support and operating within an educational framework led by human educators. Human teachers are essential in setting learning objectives, fostering student curiosity, and offering social-emotional learning that AI cannot replicate. The better you know your students, the more effectively you can steer generative AI tools to help students learn.

AI offers tailored lesson plans, activities, and assignments in line with subjects, grade levels, and student needs. AI tools like ChatGPT, Google Gemini, and Microsoft Copilot suggest lesson flows, activities, discussion questions, and assignments based on an inputted objective or topic and student characteristics. Over time, these AI systems improve the quality of their recommendations based on feedback from teachers. However, teachers and their relationships with the students provide the required human-centered, relationally-based information about what works and engages the students in learning.

As an example, consider a math teacher needing quick activities and worksheets for students struggling with fractions. Upon inputting this information into an AI lesson planning tool, she receives a range of interactive online activities, worksheets, and recommended resources for teaching fractions. These suggestions can be modified or enhanced based on the teacher's expertise and the students' needs, leading to an improved AI recommendation system over time.

Finding the ideal balance between automation and human effort is essential for successful AI integration. AI serves as a teacher assistant, offering a starting place for educators to customize the lessons, design the activities, and repurpose the course materials to engage their students.

The journey to integrating AI into your teaching practice begins with understanding the AI tools available and how they work. Now let's get familiar with some popular AI tools for education, their features, and how they can be harnessed for lesson planning and content generation. Then we'll cover tips on evaluating which AI tools are the best fit for your specific needs and teaching context.

ENHANCING LESSON PLANNING WITH AI CHATBOTS

The rise of AI has empowered technologies like ChatGPT, Google Gemini, Claude, and Microsoft Copilot—sophisticated chatbots trained to understand and generate human language. While chatbots cannot match human intelligence, they show promise for enhancing education. For example, teachers leverage these tools to provide personalized, interactive learning experiences for students.

> These tools are here to complement, not replace, your pedagogical expertise and creativity.

So, how do you gradually integrate chatbots into lesson planning and content generation?

The first area where AI chatbots can make a tangible impact is in lesson planning. As we are all well aware, crafting a lesson plan is often a time-consuming process that requires significant creativity and resourcefulness. With the help of AI chatbots, this process becomes streamlined and efficient, leaving educators with more time to engage directly with students. Here are a few ways teachers can deploy the assistance of AI:

- **AI as a Research Assistant:** Chatbots like Google Gemini and Microsoft Copilot function as highly effective research assistants. They quickly retrieve relevant information on a wide variety of topics, acting as a springboard for lesson plan ideas. For example, if you're planning a lesson on climate change, a simple prompt to these chatbots retrieves a broad spectrum of information ranging from the scientific basics of climate change to its socioeconomic impacts.
- **AI for Ideation:** With their ability to generate human-like text, chatbots serve as a tool for brainstorming and ideation. For instance, you can ask Google Gemini to generate a short story that you can use as a basis for a creative writing lesson. Similarly, ChatGPT provides various ways to approach a particular topic, helping to create a diverse and engaging lesson plan.
- **AI for Customization:** AI also assists in customizing lesson plans to cater to different learning styles and levels. For instance, you can use Microsoft Copilot to find resources or strategies for teaching complex concepts to students with different learning needs.

SUPPORTING CONTENT GENERATION WITH AI CHATBOTS

Now, let's cover content generation. Remember, these tools are here to complement, not replace, your pedagogical expertise and creativity. The goal is to harness their potential to save time, stimulate creativity, and cater to a diverse range of student needs and interests. Each of these strategies for content generation can be adjusted and customized to meet the needs of your specific educational context, adding a powerful tool to your pedagogical arsenal.

- **AI for Text Generation:** AI chatbots are useful tools for generating educational content. For example, you can prompt Google Gemini, ChatGPT, Microsoft Copilot, or Claude with a topic, and the AI creates a brief summary, a detailed explanation, or even quiz questions. This is incredibly helpful in generating teaching materials such as handouts, worksheets, or online content.
- **AI for Real-Time Interaction:** They can also be employed for creating interactive content. An example is when you set up a scenario where students interact with the chatbot to explore a topic or solve a problem. This facilitates active learning and helps students develop critical thinking skills.
- **AI for Creative Exercises:** AI chatbots stimulate creativity in students. For example, you can use Microsoft Copilot to generate a creative writing prompt or a unique problem-solving scenario.
- **AI for Multimedia Content:** They also provide valuable input for creating multimedia educational content. You can, for instance, use them to generate scripts for educational videos or to create engaging presentations with rich, relevant content.

EXPLORING AI TOOLS FOR LESSON PLANNING AND PERSONALIZED CONTENT OR CURRICULUM

Now, we get down to the details you've been waiting for: practical applications and case studies of AI-assisted lesson planning and content generation to further illustrate these strategies. AI is causing a transformative shift in education, offering powerful new possibilities for personalized and customized learning.

AI language models like ChatGPT, Google Gemini, Microsoft Copilot, and Claude are finding their place in the heart of lesson planning. These models help teachers brainstorm project ideas, generate engaging icebreaker activities, and even explain complex concepts in simple terms. The practical applications of these AI models can enhance lessons, making the content more engaging and relevant to students' needs.

Alongside lesson planning, AI also holds the potential to generate highly customized content tailored to individual learners. Leveraging what teachers know about students' needs, skill levels, interests, and more, AI tools can create everything from basic worksheets to full courses personalized for each student with the right prompts from a skilled educator. This represents a turning point for education, with adaptive, equitable learning pathways becoming a possibility for all.

Here are some ideas for using generative AI tools with students, once they've been approved by your IT team and administrators and you have parental consent (see micahminer.com for visuals of these ideas):

- **Personalized Learning:** Generate unique readings tailored to each class, group, or student. These tools also create writing prompts based on individual interests and other differentiated strategies.
- **Research Projects:** AI tools like ChatGPT assist in generating research questions and identifying sources, thus aiding students in their research process.
- **Reviews and Assessments:** Create custom quizzes and provide feedback on student responses, enabling personalized assessments that cater to each student's learning needs.
- **Vocabulary Building and Translation Support:** AI tools aid in understanding social studies vocabulary and concepts in different languages by providing definitions and examples in non-English languages.

What Strategies Will Help Me Integrate AI in These Areas Effectively?

AI tools are not meant to replace traditional teaching methods but to augment them. Here are strategies to effectively blend AI tools into your existing teaching methods, keeping the classroom experience human-centered and grounded in pedagogical best practices. The practical examples demonstrate how to balance the use of AI and traditional teaching methods in both lesson planning and content generation.

START SMALL AND BUILD UP

For teachers first exploring the use of AI in their classrooms, the best approach is to start small and build up gradually. Beginning with a single AI tool or using it for a limited task allows you to become comfortable with the technology in a low-pressure way. As your confidence grows in revising and providing feedback to improve the AI, you then slowly expand how it supports your work over time.

For example, a fourth-grade teacher may initially want to use AI only for frequent formative assessments of student learning using personalized readings with a specific vocabulary. Tools like Google Gemini offer quick reading creation of those targeted vocabulary words at the students' reading levels and create assessments with personalized feedback based on teacher prompts and student examples. The teacher could have students complete one short, personalized reading assessment per week, allowing the AI to provide instant reports on student progress and needs. The teacher reviews the results, makes notes on any areas the AI could improve, and shares individual feedback with each student.

Over the course of a month, the teacher observes how to best interpret the AI data and increasingly relies upon instant feedback to tailor instruction for the class and struggling students. The quality of the AI recommendations also improves based on the teacher's input. Feeling more at ease with the technology and confident in her ability to monitor it well, the teacher may then want to try using the weekly personalized reading assessments for follow-up work as well. The AI tool generates a customized set of practice readings and uses for the targeted vocabulary, plus AI-created artwork to support these readings and strengthen students' skills.

This type of gradual integration with continuous improvement based on teacher guidance is key. In time, as comfort levels increase, teachers may explore using additional AI tools for other areas, like lesson planning, interactive lessons, or story generation. But with each new use, start small: focus the AI on a specific task, double-check its work, modify as needed, and provide constructive feedback. Byte by byte, a well-designed and conscientious approach to integrating AI with educator oversight leads to the best outcomes for students. With care, openness, and patience, AI slowly transforms learning rather than disrupts it.

REVIEW AND REVISE

While AI tools promise to help generate ideas, recommendations, and initial drafts for educators, human judgment is still critical. Teachers know their students, goals, and subjects best. They should never use any AI-suggested content, lesson plans, or materials without reviewing and revising them first.

For example, ChatGPT may recommend a series of science experiments on the topic of light for sixth graders. The suggestions may be good but possibly incomplete, culturally biased, or too difficult for some students. The teacher reviews the recommendations and modifies them based on issues he notices. He adjusts the vocabulary in instructions for English language learners, provides alternative experiments using readily available materials for students without certain supplies at home, and includes extra explanations and diagrams for complex concepts.

> The more narrowly an AI tool is aimed at a need, the more likely it is to produce useful and relevant content or recommendations.

After the lesson, the teacher also rates the usefulness of the AI recommendations on a five-star scale and provides additional comments on improving them for his students. He then highlights parts that worked well and explains what adaptations were necessary for his class. This feedback becomes invaluable for enhancing the AI system and its suggestions over time based on the teacher's experience and needs.

It is an essential responsibility of educators using these tools to review and revise the AI output. While AI will continue advancing, it cannot yet replicate the nuanced judgment of skilled teachers in shaping learning for diverse students and ensuring equity. Its current abilities depend largely on being "trained" on massive data sets that inevitably reflect certain biases, gaps, and limitations. Teachers fill in those gaps ... but only if they double-check AI's work first.

FOCUS THE AI

For the best results from AI tools, it's important for teachers to provide constraints and guidelines to focus the technology on specific tasks. The more narrowly an AI tool is aimed at a need, the more likely it is to produce useful and relevant content or recommendations. Tap into your knowledge of your students, subjects, and learning objectives to set parameters and ensure AI meets your particular requirements.

This AIDE framework is a universal guide that is adaptable for various educational roles and objectives. It's designed to ensure you get the most accurate and useful information or materials from your AI tool (see Image 4.2 for a handy reminder and explore these concepts more on micahminer.com):

- **A = Assess the Situation:** Identify your role and what you want to achieve.
- **I = Identify the Tool's Capabilities:** Understand the tool's features and data needs.
- **D = Design the Prompt:** Create a clear, contextual prompt with guidelines.
- **E = Execute and Evaluate:** Run the prompt, review, refine, and evaluate.

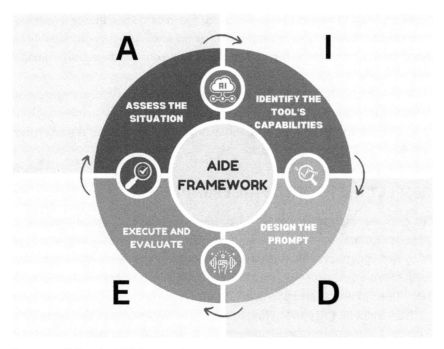

Image 4.2: Follow the AIDE framework.

For example, if a teacher wants help generating story prompts for students, she shares specifics with the AI tool ChatGPT: a particular topic (such as friendship), an approximate length or reading level, and a request for the stories to have a clear message of empowerment and inclusion. With these focused targets, the AI is able to recommend story starters far more suited to the teacher's goals than if it had simply been asked for any story prompts. The teacher may still want to review the suggestions but will likely find more directly useful ones.

When planning a history unit on the Middle Ages, a teacher may prompt an AI tool like Microsoft Copilot with the specific topics, skills, and types of lessons and activities he needs recommendations on. Examples might include lessons on the feudal system, the Magna Carta, daily life in the Middle Ages, and opportunities for students to make comparisons across time periods. With these parameters, the AI provides a customized set of relevant suggestions the teacher can select from and refine rather than some generic lessons on medieval Europe. Focusing the AI narrows in on the teacher's needs.

Some tools even allow teachers to specify details like subject, grade level, skills, topics, and types of content wanted (such as videos, interactive activities, or worksheets). The technology relies on endless data and algorithms, but it still requires human guidance and context to produce truly valuable and personalized education material.

Teachers should not feel they have to take or make use of every suggestion from AI tools. But by providing a lens through which to focus, they enable AI tools to start approximating and enhancing what they aim to do every day: inspire students to learn and grow.

RESPECT THE POWER OF THE PROMPT

It's time we explore the world of prompt engineering (sometimes called prompt crafting). As educators, we have a unique opportunity to guide these AI tools through carefully crafted prompts, coaxing out the most accurate and useful responses. However, mastering this art doesn't happen overnight—it takes time, patience, and practice.

Now imagine the power of equipping your students with this same skill. Picture a classroom where students craft prompts that help chatbots or similar technologies generate meaningful, relevant text responses. Not only does this enhance their interaction with AI, but it also sharpens their problem-solving and critical thinking skills. They aren't just waiting for the final answer ... they're actively engaged in the process, assessing the AI-generated responses every step of the way.

Using the AIDE framework, well-placed questions spark a light in students' eyes, trigger curiosity, and ignite critical thinking. Yet, how often do we pause to contemplate the crafting of these prompts themselves? Enter the fascinating realm of prompt engineering, an art form—and an essential skill—that every educator can and should master.

Constructing engaging prompts doesn't just occur by happenstance. It's akin to a master sculptor chiseling a statue from a block of marble: each prompt is intentionally molded to stimulate the kind of thinking and responses we desire from our students. Successful prompt engineering fosters a deeper connection when teachers generate personalized content for their students based on their relationship and understanding of what interests these students.

Another vital skill is teaching students to prompt an AI tool as part of learning the content, cultivating high-quality work and a profound level of engagement. As a bonus, this grants us, the educators, valuable insight into our students' thought processes, which shapes our instruction (if we teach good questions and have the students document their learning). As we all know, making learning visible is a best practice in education, and this is one way to teach students the art of good questions.

Most educators reading this are new to the idea of prompt engineering, but fear not! The trick is to start simple. Focus on the verbs in your prompts. Verbs such as "identify," "describe," and "explain" encourage students to display surface-level understanding, while power verbs like "argue," "critique," and "analyze" elicit deeper, more analytical engagement. Don't forget to consider the content and complexity of your prompts. They should be accessible yet sufficiently challenging to stimulate our students' cognitive capabilities.

Effective prompts are a fine balance of context and constraints that shepherd educators' and students' thinking without becoming excessively restrictive. They should also allow for student choice and individual voice. Think about how you craft an open-ended prompt that orbits around your learning objectives, guiding students in a general direction but not confining them to a single correct answer.

REMEMBER: AI FOR IDEAS, HUMANS FOR CREATIVITY

While AI tools show promise for generating ideas, recommendations, and initial drafts to assist teachers, human creativity, vetting, and judgment remain essential. Educators know how to shape learning for their students in ways that also nurture creativity, empathy, and social-emotional growth. They tap into both expertise and intuition to creatively adapt resources for learners on their journey to becoming independent thinkers and caring citizens.

Here's an example: An AI tool like Google Gemini may suggest a basic lesson plan on persuasive writing for eighth graders that includes an essay outline template and rubric. A teacher reviews this plan, sees potential, and sees opportunities to enhance creative thinking. She adapts the outline to be less prescriptive and more open-ended, allowing students to select from a list of possible ways to begin and end an essay. She also adds opportunities for students to peer review and provide collective feedback to one another as writers.

The teacher notices the rubric focuses heavily on structure, grammar, and vocabulary. She modifies it to equally emphasize originality, voice, and passion for the topic. Students are encouraged to not just follow a formula but push the boundaries of the assignment. The teacher also plans to read and discuss a highly persuasive speech to demonstrate how writers make emotional connections with readers.

While the original AI-suggested lesson plan was helpful as a starting point, the teacher tapped into her creativity and knowledge of her students to improve it. She shaped the plan to align with goals beyond just mechanical skills, nurturing student imagination and motivation. This kind of adaptation based on human judgment is key. AI cannot replicate an educator's ability to emotionally inspire learners or think critically about what skills they need for life beyond any one lesson.

Teachers will always be essential for enabling students to grow, not just in knowledge but in creativity. They show learners how to remix and reimagine by doing so themselves. While tools may generate templates, educators steer learning as a creative endeavor full of possibility. AI inspires new paths; educators walk them with students while building dreams along the way.

MONITOR, MODIFY, AND PROVIDE FEEDBACK

Simply integrating AI tools into teaching practice is not enough. Educators must closely monitor how these tools support students and make modifications as needed to ensure the best results. They should also provide regular feedback to help systems continue learning and improving over time.

Just like students, AI tools benefit substantially from teacher guidance. The prompts and questions teachers use to create the content can be modified based on educators' reviews and insights into how well assessments measure intended skills. If students seem to struggle with particular questions or show unexpected knowledge gaps, teachers determine if the issues lie with the questions themselves or whether they reveal opportunities to strengthen instruction. Detailed feedback helps transform assessments into a useful gauge of progress.

While imperfect, AI inspires new forms of responsive teaching; tools that used to be one-size-fits-all are now personalized for each student. Vast amounts of data inform, but human insight guides. Together, they unlock new freedoms for learners and educators to go where curiosity leads. The future of education with AI is one of partnership and possibility. Monitor, modify, and always keep sight of why we educate: to empower dreams beyond all that's been built before.

NOTE: With many companies creating AI tools for education, teachers must determine which options align with their needs and values. It's important to evaluate different tools based on factors like validity, ethics, bias, usefulness for diverse students, and level of teacher control and flexibility. The technology used inevitably shapes learning, for better or worse. Educators can demand AI that keeps student data private, considers equity, and allows teachers to guide how tools are used.

BRING IT ALL TOGETHER

While AI opens up new possibilities for education that are personalized, engaging, and scalable, human educators remain essential for guiding how these tools are developed and applied. Teachers understand students, learning, and subjects in ways that AI cannot match. But when integrated thoughtfully under the guidance of compassionate educators, AI may enhance how we inspire young minds.

The LEAP Framework in a General Education Classroom

Here are a few short examples of the LEAP application for AI tech integration with the AIDE framework.

Scenario 1

LEARNER-CENTERED APPROACH IN PROJECT-BASED LEARNING

Ms. Johnson, a middle school science teacher, wanted to engage her students in a project-based learning module about ecosystems. To kick off the project, she used ChatGPT to generate a list of diverse ecosystems, from tundras to tropical rainforests, from which her students could choose.

Let's run this through the AIDE prompting framework:

A: ASSESS THE SITUATION

Role: Ms. Johnson is a middle school science teacher.

Objective: She aims to kick-start a project-based learning module on ecosystems and wants to provide her students with a diverse list of ecosystems to choose from for their projects.

I: IDENTIFY THE TOOL'S CAPABILITIES

Tool: ChatGPT.

Features: The tool generates lists, provides detailed descriptions, and even suggests project ideas.

Data Needs: The tool performs best when given a clear, specific prompt.

D: DESIGN THE PROMPT

Prompt: "Generate a list of ten diverse ecosystems, ranging from tundras to tropical rainforests. Include a two- to three-sentence description for each, highlighting its key features and why it would be an interesting choice for a middle school science project on ecosystems."

E: EXECUTE AND EVALUATE

Run the Prompt: Ms. Johnson inputs the designed prompt into ChatGPT.

Review: She reviews the generated list and descriptions to ensure they are scientifically accurate and engaging for middle school students.

Refine: If needed, Ms. Johnson adjusts the list or adds supplemental information.

Evaluate: Once the list is distributed and projects are underway, Ms. Johnson measures student engagement and understanding to assess the effectiveness of using the AI-generated list.

AND NOW THE LEAP FRAMEWORK:

Learner-Centered: Ms. Johnson incorporates student choice in project topics, putting the focus on their individual learning paths and interests.

Ethical Adoption: She reviews and verifies the information generated by ChatGPT to ensure its accuracy and appropriateness.

Adaptive Personalization: By allowing students to select their ecosystem, the project becomes tailored to each student's interests.

Performance Reflection: Ms. Johnson gathers feedback and evaluates the project's outcome, reflecting on how effectively the AI tool enhances learner-centered education in her classroom.

Scenario 2

ETHICAL ADOPTION IN A LANGUAGE CLASSROOM

Mr. Lopez, a high school Spanish teacher, is looking for new ways to make his dialogues more engaging. He decides to use Google Gemini to create dialogue scenarios for his students, ranging from ordering food in a restaurant to discussing environmental issues.

Let's run this through AIDE:

A: ASSESS

Role: Mr. Lopez is a high school Spanish teacher.

Objective: Create engaging dialogue scenarios for students.

I: IDENTIFY

Tool: Google Gemini.

Features: Generates dialogue scenarios based on prompts.

Data Needs: Gemini can work with your Google Docs, use the internet to complete questions, and help with translations when clearly prompted.

D: DESIGN

Prompt: "Generate five dialogue scenarios for high school Spanish students. Topics should range from ordering food in a restaurant to discussing environmental issues."

E: EXECUTE AND EVALUATE

Run: Input prompt into Google Gemini.

Review: Check dialogues for appropriateness and educational value.

Refine: Make any needed edits.

Evaluate: Use in class and monitor student engagement.

NOW, APPLY IT TO THE LEAP FRAMEWORK:

Learner-Centered: The AI-generated scenarios provide an opportunity for students to practice language skills in a variety of real-world contexts.

Ethical Adoption: Mr. Lopez carefully reviews and edits the AI-generated dialogues to ensure they are culturally sensitive and don't reinforce stereotypes.

Adaptive Personalization: He then adapts dialogues to match different proficiency levels, ensuring every student can effectively engage with the material.

Performance Reflection: Over the term, Mr. Lopez evaluates his students' progress, collects feedback on the scenarios, and adjusts as necessary to optimize their language learning.

Scenario 3

PERFORMANCE REFLECTION IN SOCIAL STUDIES

Mr. Patel, a social studies teacher, incorporates AI into his lesson planning and content generation to diversify and enrich his students' learning experience. Using ChatGPT, he generates content on various historical events and social issues.

Once again, let's review with the AIDE guide:

A: ASSESS

Role: Mr. Patel, social studies teacher.

Objective: Diversify and enrich content on historical events and social issues.

I: IDENTIFY

Tool: ChatGPT.

Features: Generates text on a wide range of topics, including historical events and social issues.

Data Needs: If you pay for ChatGPT 4, then you have access to plug-ins, DALL-E 3, Data Analyst to help with analysis, and Custom GPTs to help with your prompting; if you are using the free version, create a clear, targeted prompt with specific parameters.

D: DESIGN

Prompt: "Generate summaries and discussion questions for five key historical events and social issues relevant to this semester's curriculum."

E: EXECUTE AND EVALUATE

Run: Input the prompt into ChatGPT.

Review: Check the generated content for accuracy and educational depth.

Refine: Edit or supplement as needed.

Execute and Evaluate: Implement in class and assess student engagement and understanding.

AND LET'S LEAP ONCE MORE:

Learner-Centered: Mr. Patel uses AI to broaden the range of content available to students, making their learning experience more engaging and enriching.

Ethical Adoption: He's mindful of student privacy and equity while using the AI tool.

Adaptive Personalization: The AI tool generates diverse content, keeping the material engaging and adaptable to various learning styles.

Performance Reflection: Mr. Patel reflects on the effectiveness of this approach by assessing student engagement, learning outcomes, and feedback, making necessary adjustments to improve the learning experience.

REBOOT

AI is poised to revolutionize how educators efficiently and creatively plan impactful learning experiences every day. It has the power to suggest tailored lessons, streamline planning, and make the important but time-consuming work of curriculum and learning design much more sustainable and scalable. By understanding the potential of AI and learning to harness it effectively, we can chart the course toward a future where technology and human ingenuity work side-by-side, creating enriched educational experiences for all students.

For educators, the ideal approach is to view generative AI as a tool for good teaching practices. AI-generated content and curriculum can be used as resources to enhance educators' expertise. Teachers filter, evaluate, and select the best AI-generated materials that align with their goals while also monitoring how students are progressing through the customized content. Their guidance, feedback, and encouragement ensure that with the oversight and support of caring teachers, AI helps create a thriving personalized ecosystem for students.

The key is to begin thoughtfully, and then evolve responsibly. Whether you're just getting started with a single AI tool or looking to expand the role of technology in your teaching, build up and innovate with careful intention, not for technology's sake but because you know your students and their goals. By leading with compassion, you guide AI to serve and amplify what matters most: empowered learning, creative expression, and growth for every child.

With regular feedback from educators focused on specific student needs, AI systems improve in providing more relevant, high-quality material. However, teachers must stay closely involved as monitors, editors, and supporters of student learning. They know AI cannot be relied upon alone to get it right or to inspire young minds. Teachers motivate students; AI motivates teachers. And together, they enhance how we personalize education.

Chapter 5
Teaching with AI for a Human-Centered Approach

AI has been climbing the ladder of cognitive abilities for decades, and it now looks set to reach human-level performance across a very wide range of tasks within the next three years.

— *Mustafa Suleyman, cofounder of DeepMind and author of* The Coming Wave

Image 5.1: Embracing AI in the classroom doesn't mean leaving humanity behind.

O kay, let's dive into proven educational practices that amplify critical thinking skills in students—a key component of preparing them for a future where AI and other technologies could easily become normalized. It's no secret that these skills are a hot commodity in today's job market, yet they're often in short supply. Why the discrepancy? Research tells us that employers place a higher value on workers who can think critically rather than on those equipped with technical skills alone. And for good reason: critical thinking equips students to scrutinize information objectively, make logical decisions, and address complex problems—competencies that are vital in our increasingly intricate world.

How Can My Teaching Stay Human-Centered with AI?

Let's refamiliarize ourselves with how we can nurture critical thinking skills in the classroom. All of these time-tested and important teaching practices can be supported, co-created, and scaffolded by AI tools like ChatGPT, Claude, Google Gemini, Microsoft Copilot, and others, but none of the practices can be replaced by AI tools in the classroom. This is how we keep our teaching and learning human-centered.

ASKING QUESTIONS: THE CATALYST FOR CRITICAL THINKING, AI EDITION

We know asking questions sparks learning and critical thinking. In classrooms, the simple act of students wondering *why* or *what if* ignites discussion, exposes gaps in understanding, and inspires new insights. Now imagine adding AI to the mix. AI tools can pump fuel into this question-powered learning engine, helping teachers and students strengthen higher-level thinking skills through open-ended inquiry.

For teachers, AI provides ways to craft thought-provoking yet strategic questions, the hallmark of the Socratic questioning method. AI-based discussion platforms suggest open-ended questions beginning with *why*, *how*, and *what if* to spark engaging answers and deeper thinking. They offer follow-up questions for students' responses to probe their logic and consider different angles.

Students also need to develop questioning skills by framing their own inquiries. AI facilitates this through interactive platforms where students post questions, get responses, ask follow-ups, and vote on the most thought-provoking questions. An AI-enabled *question wall* encourages students to examine assumptions, consider alternative views, and gain new insights as their questions and discussions become more complex over time.

With AI, your students' curiosity powers a self-perpetuating cycle of learning. Their questions lead to answers as well as new questions in an open-ended flow of ideas, while AI tools provide the structure to guide discussions productively. Students realize questions have merit not merely for eliciting answers but for exposing more dimensions of truth waiting to be revealed through continued exploration.

Over time, students' thinking evolves from superficial to nuanced, transcending the status quo boundaries. Comfort with ambiguity grows as they value questions that challenge preconceptions over those with definitive answers. They gain a questioning mindset where inquiry becomes a default method of navigating uncertainty on their path to understanding and purpose.

> By merging human and artificial elements to foster questioning, we give students an enduring gift: the capacity for self-directed learning.

Teachers cultivate this environment by valuing all questions equally and showing how AI can enhance learning through strategic questioning and discussion. While AI generates suggested questions and routes for open-ended dialogue, the human connection—between teachers, students, and ideas—remains essential. When powered by curiosity and a partnership with AI, students discover their potential to chart meaning, find purpose, and thrive in a complex world through continual questioning and openness to new understanding.

By merging human and artificial elements to foster questioning, we give students an enduring gift: the capacity for self-directed learning. AI becomes not an end in itself but a means of amplifying human potential for creative thought, empathy, and progress. And through the simple act of wondering together, we take a step closer to wisdom.

Critical thinking is the cornerstone of education, preparing our students to navigate an increasingly complex world. In our digital era, AI offers us powerful tools to augment this essential skill. Image 5.2 illustrates how we can harness AI to foster a culture of inquiry, exploration, and wisdom in our classrooms without losing the irreplaceable human connection that makes education truly transformative.

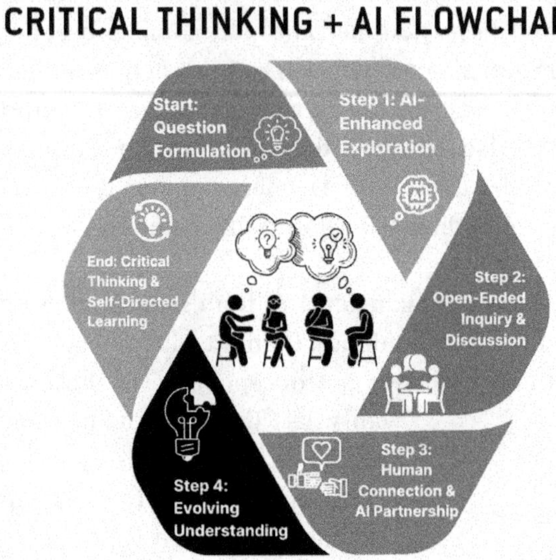

CRITICAL THINKING + AI FLOWCHART

Image 5.2

INCORPORATING ANALOGIES: A POWERFUL BRIDGE BETWEEN CONCEPTS

Remember those SAT analogies? They aren't just useful for test preparation; they are an invaluable teaching tool that helps students build connections between familiar and unfamiliar ideas. Analogies encourage students to think broadly and logically, strengthening their understanding by creating conceptual bridges. AI is great at helping you come up with analogies that work with your lesson plans and vocabulary. Even though analogies are a human-centered pedagogical concept, AI can help promote human-centered critical thinking by helping educators make analogies for students for almost any learning.

In education, analogies serve as a secret weapon for developing critical thinking skills. When students map relationships between two complex concepts, they cultivate abilities that will propel their learning for years to come. Strong analogies require students to evaluate similarities and differences, determine what makes them comparable, and synthesize these relationships—all while exercising their cognitive muscles. AI can assist with brainstorming unique ways to use analogies to help students make connections and think critically.

For example, to understand how the solar system works, students compare the revolution of planets around the sun to the movements of the hands of a clock. The sun acts as the center point, while the planets move at different rates like the hour, minute, and second hands. This simple yet illuminating analogy conveys why planets closer to the sun move more quickly. But sometimes teachers may not have the time to find and think about how to make this point clear to students. AI can assist with these kinds of support for analogies in seconds, saving teachers time and helping students learn.

Or when teaching the water cycle, you compare it to another continuous process, such as a bustling factory production line. Explain how there is a certain flow (ha!) to how water molecules change form that can be attributed to—and is essential for—the cooling, purification, distribution, and development of life on Earth. If you need help or examples to promote understanding or find ways to see how important the water cycle is for students in different relevant ways, AI can do this quickly and effectively for any teacher at any time.

Teachers can use analogies across subjects and age levels to build students' understanding and spark insights. Start with simple analogies and progress to more complex relationships over time as critical thinking skills develop. But don't just use analogies as an explanation technique—have students create their own to demonstrate their thinking. Ask: "What analogy would you make to represent how our system of government works?" or "How is the process of cell division similar to something in the everyday world?" That is where AI comes in to help you brainstorm ideas and ways to reinforce or help raise great questions.

By employing AI to help teachers with analogies strategically and often in your teaching, you build comprehension and the cognitive capacity for logical reasoning and relational thinking in your students. These skills are universally important ways to promote human-centered critical thinking, and AI can help sharpen these ideas to help humans learn them. Students' futures will be brighter for it, and they will be more prepared to understand complex systems and make connections, which is an important attribute for thinking critically, even in a technology-driven future full of more AI tools.

INITIATING INTERACTIONS:
THE SECRET INGREDIENT OF CRITICAL THINKING

Lively interaction and discussion are essential for cultivating students' critical thinking abilities. Without the exchange of ideas, critical thinking cannot develop. Group discussions, collaborative work, and peer interactions provide the perfect backdrop for exercising and strengthening students' cognitive muscles. AI can help teachers create sentence stems, raise questions, and find useful ways to start and maintain collaborative group discussions.

When students engage with others, they must explain their reasoning, ask thoughtful questions, evaluate different perspectives, bridge discrepancies, and (in some cases) revise their initial thinking. These skills—communication, negotiation, thinking on your feet, finding common ground—are profoundly useful in the classroom and in life. AI tools are great for teachers to promote different perspectives, create questions for deeper knowledge and connections, support divergent thinking when needed, and play the devil's advocate to challenge assumptions in thinking.

For example, staging debates on current events gives students opportunities to craft persuasive arguments, pose analytical questions, and consider alternative viewpoints, all of which hone critical thinking skills. Assign collaborative projects where students must work together to solve open-ended problems. This fosters creativity, compromise, and higher-level thinking about complex issues as students navigate challenges together. AI can help with debates: you can debate the AI tool, use AI to prepare students for debates, or raise ideas for Socratic Seminars. It can assist teachers with posing leveled questions, tiering current questions, promoting creativity in tackling unique problems, or creating ethical dilemmas to help students grapple with complex issues.

Even simple pair-share activities where students explore each other's ideas provide benefits. As students articulate thoughts through discussion, their thinking gains depth, nuance, and sophistication. Peer interactions also broaden students' intellectual reach as they encounter different ways of understanding concepts. Your creative assistant in creating pair-share activities can be AI. Want ideas for collaborative bell ringers or transition activities? AI can help you with that.

With mindful facilitation, interaction gives rise to creativity, cognitive flexibility, and higher-level thinking that would not emerge in isolation. Students grow increasingly skillful in examining issues from multiple angles and explaining ideas coherently. When this is done well over time, they develop an ability to reason logically in response to different and even opposing viewpoints. Teachers can use AI to incorporate more ways to provide this balance and nuance in perspectives.

Fusing interaction and critical thinking should be a top priority in any classroom. When students engage regularly in stimulating discussions and collaborations, they discover their intellectual potential through a multidimensional process of sharing, questioning, debating, and revising ideas collectively. This mindset that values openness, evidence, and logical reasoning then moves with them beyond schooling to shape a lifetime of pursuing truth. AI tools can inspire, support, and promote these interactions, helping teachers cultivate knowledge and wisdom in their students, one discussion at a time. The thinking that results holds promise for shaping a better and more just world. Though not technically magic, higher-level thinking has the power to transform learning.

By weaving these strategies into your lesson plans, you're teaching students a subject while preparing them for an increasingly complex world that could be filled with AI and countless other technological breakthroughs that can be used for good or bad. You're equipping them with the ability to think critically, question thoroughly, and solve problems creatively with AI as your teacher assistant. And that, my friends, is how we empower our future generations. (To view a self-assessment rubric, check out micahminer.com.)

LEVELING UP: ENHANCING PEER INTERACTIONS WITH AI

Embracing generative AI tools in the classroom enriches content and elevates the ways students interact and engage with one another. AI supports various interaction activities—from debates to pair-shares—and fosters critical thinking. By leveraging AI, educators can create dynamic, responsive, and insightful learning experiences that adapt to students' needs and stimulate deeper intellectual growth. Whether it's providing evidence for debates or tailoring peer interactions, generative AI offers a versatile set of tools that teachers and students can harness to complement human creativity and empathy, making education more personalized and effective.

Peer Interaction Enhanced with AI Tools:

- **Broadens Interactions:** AI tailors peer interactions to enhance understanding and broaden perspectives.

- **Fosters Different Perspectives:** AI offers diverse perspectives and evidence, enriching debate quality.
- **Facilitates Deeper Discussions:** AI facilitates rich discussions by providing insights and encouraging deeper exploration.
- **Improves Communication:** AI prompts encourage engaging conversations, enhancing communication skills.
- **Supports Teamwork:** AI supports teamwork, fosters creativity, and guides project organization.

GAINING TIME: AI AS AN ADMINISTRATIVE ASSISTANT

Imagine an AI that can generate personalized lesson plans tailored to each student's needs while adapting the content, pace, and style for optimal learning. What an incredible gift for time-strapped teachers! When AI helps with planning and assessment, educators have more free time to focus on what really matters: nurturing students.

Still, AI is only as effective as the data and algorithms that power it. Its knowledge and recommendations are limited by what we teach it. AI cannot replicate the insight, intuition, and care that teachers provide.

Rather than only relying on AI, you must guide its development. Work with AI as a partner: evaluate its suggestions, provide feedback, and use your own expertise to refine its skills and content. That way, its knowledge continues to strengthen in service to real students and classrooms. Teachers remain essential in crafting AI to be useful, fair, and aligned with our values.

CRAFTING CHATBOTS: A THOUGHT EXPERIMENT

AI is revolutionizing our lives, including in the field of education. The promise of emerging AI tools like Character.ai (an advanced neural network chatbot) is fascinating. Such AI tools, still in the early stages as this book goes to print, hint at the potential to extend the reach of education centered on learners. It is also important to realize how and where these emerging AI tools can be applied thoughtfully and where they should not be used. While there is a concern that biases could be built into bots if not developed thoughtfully, the chance to teach students about how these technologies work shows promise.

To better understand current capabilities and limits, I created the experimental Minerclass Beta chatbot and shared my thoughts on responsible integration of these tools in K–12 education. Training the AI chatbot was relatively simple: I created 109 questions and answers about different characteristics I wanted the chatbot to be an expert in—including motivating students and general knowledge of history and literature—and tested it with a volunteer group of middle school social studies teachers in my district. Minerclass Beta is fun, knows basic history facts, and doesn't go off the rails, but it's not ready for prime time with students. It would, however, be a great tool to teach about AI literacy and awareness so students can slowly learn how to use the tools and demystify AI.

So, how might teacher-crafted chatbots assist students?

- Provide immediate feedback and answers to common queries
- Share resources for learning
- Deliver mini-lessons or learning activities
- Reinforce key concepts
- Offer supportive guidance
- Personalize information to students' needs

In the future—with the proper safeguards, guardrails, and setups, as well as teachers shaping their development and use—chatbots could provide quick feedback, engage students, and share resources to support learning, even beyond the classroom. SchoolAI is a platform that attempts to meet these expectations, among others. At the time of this writing, edtech experts don't recommend using AI as a verified representation of you as the teacher. However, in the future, this capability may be ready and useful for both teachers and students.

The crucial point here is that teachers drive the application of any AI tool, including chatbots, to meet students' needs. With teachers' wisdom, expertise, and care, these tools provide enhanced support for learners while freeing up teachers to focus on nurturing interactions that technology alone can't replicate. Remember, the better you know your students—their hobbies, their interests, and their academic strengths and weaknesses—the more impactful leveraging AI will be for the students, and the more human-centered their learning can be.

What Strategies Ensure This Balance between AI Capabilities and Human Education?

AI promises efficiency in the classroom by grading assignments quickly, adapting lessons, and answering questions. But efficiency isn't always effective. AI can't teach students to ask good questions, provoke thought, or inspire a lifelong love of learning ... that's what teachers do.

The key is finding the right balance.

Use AI for routine administrative tasks to save time for teaching, but keep human connection at the heart of learning. Engage students, spark curiosity, and instill the skills they need beyond school.

AI is a helpful tool but lacks human creativity. We can combine the best of both: AI tools help generate relevant content and materials, and then you vet the information and ideas and provide feedback. In that way, human creativity fuels discussions, projects, and an environment where innovation thrives. Together, AI and teachers achieve more.

For example, AI tailors content to student needs, but teachers possess insight that AI cannot match. Use AI to gather data on performance, preferences, and progress. Interpret it with your understanding of each student's strengths, interests, and goals. The result? Personalized learning with AI precision and human empathy.

Teachers, as we embrace AI, our mission stays the same: give students a great education for school and for life. We're not here to be replaced by AI but to use it as a tool to enhance our impact. AI can empower students ... if it is shaped by you.

With that in mind, here are a few recommendations:

- Help colleagues build confidence in AI by sharing stories of small wins and challenges. Connect over concerns about technology and talk through how to shape it around human needs. Reduce their fear of technology by focusing on how it enhances teaching rather than replaces it.
- Stay up-to-date with data privacy laws and review student data use policies. Discuss any concerns about how AI tools collect, store, and share information.
- Set clear rules around how AI collects and uses your students' data. Demand transparency and accountability to ensure tools align with the values of privacy, ethics, and student well-being.

- Review and approve AI recommendations before incorporating them into your classroom. You are responsible for the tools and methods you use. Make sure that any generative AI tools are first approved by your school leadership and technology departments. Then monitor them for negative impacts on inclusion or achievement gaps.
- Use AI tools to free up time for more human interactions like creative work, collaboration, and relationship-building. This gives you valuable time to discuss the Big Questions of life with your students.
- Share feedback with AI developers to help them understand the realities of teaching. But reserve the right to choose if and how you work with AI in your classroom. You know your students' and school's needs best, and you should be empowered to make those decisions.
- Focus your own training on enhancing human-centered skills. Develop confidence and experience in balancing high-tech and high-touch. Learn to spot where AI complements teaching and where human connection is most crucial. Build expertise in the trustworthy, responsible, and equitable use of AI.

The field of AI is rapidly evolving, and so our approach to integrating it into our teaching practices should be dynamic and adaptive. Remember to utilize the LEAP guidelines for AI tech integration in your classroom:

Although innovations inspire, our work remains the same: teach hearts and minds to soar.

- **Learner-Centered:** Our students remain the focal point. While AI tools invigorate learning and support project-based teaching, they are here to augment the learning experience, not replace human interaction.
- **Ethical Adoption:** We must stay committed to equity, inclusion, and data privacy. Any signs of bias or inappropriateness in AI tool interactions must be promptly identified and dealt with while we meticulously safeguard student data.
- **Adaptive Personalization:** AI tools can adapt to students' unique learning needs, but their suggestions should serve as a guide for our decisions, not make them for us.
- **Performance Reflection:** The key is regular evaluation of these tools' impact on learning outcomes, student experience, privacy, and equity.

The LEAP Framework in a General Education Classroom

In the ever-evolving field of AI, you must always be ready to LEAP into action, focusing on a Learner-Centered approach, ensuring Ethical Adoption, engaging in Adaptive Personalization, and conducting regular Performance Reflections. Here are a few stories of AI blending with human interaction:

- Ms. Smith was an English teacher who epitomized the Learner-Centered approach. She introduced a tool called Quillbot, which didn't require a sign-in for students, to help them with their writing and to provide feedback on the writing and grammar. She then asked students to reflect on how that AI tool helped with their writing process. Next, Ms. Smith worked with ChatGPT to give more formative feedback on student writing after they submitted the first draft, yet she made sure to discuss the AI-generated feedback personally with each student to build a trusting relationship. The students incorporated this feedback into their final drafts. As a bonus, the automated process to get feedback about all of her students not only saved Ms. Smith time but also led to a deep conversation about student growth, increasing human interaction in teaching.

- Then there's Mr. Garcia, a science teacher, who embodies the principle of Adaptive Personalization. He employed Google Gemini to target his instructional activities for small groups to support student knowledge gaps and align lessons accordingly. Mr. Garcia also used Google Gemini to help him create activities and rubrics that accommodated his students' different reading levels. This tool translated the readings for some ESL students to help measure how much they knew about the topic, not how much English they understood. Mr. Garcia knew his students well, and his human touch was evident as he designed hands-on experiments based on his understanding of his students' struggles, using AI suggestions as a guide, not a decision-maker.

- The principle of Ethical Adoption is significant in the AI era, and Mrs. Herra learned to be a pro at it. As a high school social studies teacher, she created Socratic Seminars for her students after having them research AI's impact on society for her current events unit. She used Microsoft Copilot to help brainstorm the rubric and research activities. Mrs. Herra's students discussed AI ethics based on the EU AI Law and the US AI Bill of Rights as part of their primary source research and provided ideas on setting clear rules for data collection and use as well as privacy guidelines. The class learned that it's essential to be transparent when using AI tools and for these tools to align with equity, diversity, and privacy.

- Last, Performance Reflection is a vital step in AI integration, including the consistent and ongoing evaluation of an AI tool's impact on learning outcomes, student experiences, and inclusivity. All the teachers previously mentioned reflected on their lesson planning processes that were infused with AI tools. Their conclusions? AI gave them time to focus on student capacity and relationship-building and provided students with opportunities to think critically while still being held accountable for their work.

REBOOT

Teachers, to use AI well, we must keep learning. By actively upskilling, you're building knowledge, learning new tools, and balancing them with your teaching.

But this must be ongoing work. As AI evolves, we must adapt. It may feel daunting, but we can build support from our administration, our colleagues, our students, their families, and the education community at large.

Here's my best advice:

- **Focus on emotional and social learning:** AI enhances teaching but can't replicate understanding emotions or relationships.
- **Model and teach emotional intelligence:** Discuss empathy, compassion, and ethics continuously in your classroom, in the hallways, and on the playground.
- **Equip your critical thinking instructional toolbox to instill human values:** AI can't teach kindness, respect, honesty, or responsibility ... that's part of your job.
- **Celebrate our humanity while embracing AI's benefits to enhance our learning:** It's not either/or but better together.

AI-enabled tools provide the structure to strengthen essential questioning skills in a classroom culture where inquiry is commonplace and valued. But the human connections within remain pivotal. When teachers inspire questions and train students to explore ideas through respectful dialogue, they empower them with a way of navigating the world that no technology alone could replicate.

While rapid change stirs dreams of *virtual tutors* as constant *intellectual thought partners* or *thinking buddies,* education concerns living, breathing hearts and minds, not data alone. No algorithm fulfills a mentor's role or understands students as profoundly as the guiding hands and hearts walking beside them. We must advocate for humanity guiding progress in education. Although innovations inspire, our work remains the same: teach hearts and minds to soar. Although tools may aid, the calling lights our way.

Let's go forward thoughtfully, safely embracing the promise of AI. Remember that we must steer the generative AI tools we use rather than be steered by them. Together, we have the wisdom and care to shape a future enhanced by technology while remaining centered on the human relationships that give life deep meaning. The future remains open ... and it's ours to guide.

Chapter 6
Rethinking Pedagogical Approaches in the AI Era

Change is the law of life, and those who look only to the past and present are certain to miss the future.

— *John F. Kennedy, former US president*

Image 6.1: When pen meets pixel—AI's impact on traditional instruction and assessment.

The rapid surge of AI in the educational sphere feels like we're all aboard a high-speed bullet train. With new landscapes in assessment techniques, such as automated essay scoring and plagiarism detection plus data-driven analysis of student progress, we're not just heading toward the future—we're rocketing toward it. But we're also approaching steep challenges: bias, privacy, and the risk of reducing the beautiful, multidimensional process of learning into a sterile game of numbers and percentages.

The secret, fellow educator, is to steer this train deftly, ensuring we're using technology wisely and not outsourcing our choices to AI tools. Educators know their students and what teaching and learning should be. The beauty of AI is that we can leverage it to increase teacher time with students, build relationships, and discover student interests so we can personalize content, increasing student engagement and leveling up their learning.

How Does AI Impact Traditional Teaching?

With mindful and vigilant use, AI has the potential to turn formative assessment and learning into a more engaging, almost-human experience. Now, don't get me wrong: for high-stakes assessments and growth that go beyond textbooks, there's no substitute for that old-world charm, the human touch.

How can we, as teachers, tame this AI beast to serve our goals, particularly when it comes to assessments?

Student involvement is key in this new learning dynamic. By engaging students in setting learning goals, determining assessment criteria, and deciding on the roles of AI versus human judgment, we foster an ethical and socially responsible approach to technology. For AI to empower us as educators, it needs to play the role of a handy assistant who eases routine tasks, boosts digital literacy, encourages self-assessment, and upholds academic integrity.

It's also time to rethink the traditional formats of assessment. Let's aim for a more authentic, diversified approach where students can express their understanding in numerous ways, such as presentations, conferences, and even artistic creations. AI lends a helping hand in this process, offering feedback and suggesting improvements. Approaching writing and other communication projects as a process, with incremental steps and feedback, is an effective alternative to a more traditional writing assignment, and it's also more aligned with an AI-infused world. It avoids the pitfalls of students using AI tools unethically and not being held accountable for their work.

Drawing from the wisdom of the World Economic Forum's insights on AI in education (2023), let's leverage this powerful tool to navigate the uncharted waters of tomorrow's learning landscapes. Together, we guide our ship toward a brighter future for our students.

TEACHING WRITING WITH AI

The dawn of artificial intelligence has initiated a transformative era in education and the broader spectrum of written communication. In her thoughtful article "6 Tenets of Postplagiarism: Writing in the Age of Artificial Intelligence,"

> For AI to empower us as educators, it needs to play the role of a handy assistant who eases routine tasks, boosts digital literacy, encourages self-assessment, and upholds academic integrity.

Dr. Sarah Elaine Eaton sheds light on this profound shift, urging us to reimagine our notions of creativity, language, responsibility, and intellectual ownership. This is a new and highly debated topic, and the world of education must acknowledge that we are in a new place in the evolution of writing, and we must set new guidelines.

Every silver lining has a cloud, and AI tools and chatbots in writing instruction are no different. Let's dive into a few potential issues addressed by Dr. Eaton that might ruffle our educational feathers:

- The Copy-Paste Conundrum: AI-generated content is sneaky—it makes plagiarism harder to detect and leads us into the murky waters of academic honesty. The technology is brilliant, but so are our students, right?

  AI-generated content, while remarkable in its sophistication, may blur the boundaries of academic honesty. The increasing prevalence of AI-authored content could potentially lead to instances of intended and unintended dishonesty among students. As educators, we must tread carefully in this new frontier and instill in our students the importance of original thought and effort.

- **The AI Overdose:** There's a chance that our young learners might get a tad too comfy with their AI companions. We don't want to stifle their budding writing skills, do we?

  Technology can be addictive for anyone. There's a risk that students may over-rely on AI tools, hampering the development of their independent writing skills. It's crucial that we strike the right balance. While AI tools provide guidance and feedback, they should supplement, not replace, the individual effort required to hone writing skills.

- **The AI Oopsies:** AI writing tools aren't perfect. Did we verify the information (or did our students) before we used it as an assignment or as part of a lesson plan?

  AI tools may produce inaccurate or downright nonsensical content (these are the hallucinations we covered in Chapter 2). Keep an eye out for these hiccups when blending AI into your lesson plans. Always vet and verify AI tools' responses to your prompts when you use them as intellectual thought partners or brainstorm buddies.

- **Unequal Opportunities:** Are there hidden (or maybe not-so-hidden) biases in these AI tools?

  As educators, we must ensure equal access to new technologies like AI writing aids. Gaps in student access or understanding create disparities in learning opportunities. Providing classroom technology and training for both teachers and students on these tools helps close this divide, but we must also recognize biases embedded in AI systems and mitigate their impact. With vigilance and proactive steps, we can harness the power of AI equitably.

ADDRESSING THE CHALLENGES

Ensuring equity of access and learning opportunities with AI is no easy feat. But thoughtful integration of these tools into instruction can help. We must acknowledge the AI benefits for our students while also recognizing and mitigating their shortcomings.

Here are steps you can take to address some of these challenges:

- Set clear rules for how your students utilize AI tools responsibly.
- Monitor how they are using and interacting with the tools.

- Refine your teaching practices so students continue building core writing skills, with or without AI assistance.
- Focus on using AI as a supplement rather than a substitute for human instruction and feedback.

By creating an environment that allows AI to complement our teaching rather than dictate it, we foster a classroom culture that encourages original thought, nurtures writing skills, and champions fair and equal access to technology. The key is balancing student access to AI with guidance to use it constructively and ethically. This is a fine balance, and as educators, we are well-equipped to tread this line, ensuring that the AI tools we integrate into our classrooms empower all students to reach their full potential.

NAVIGATING THE OPPORTUNITIES AND PERILS OF AI IN WRITING INSTRUCTION

We are in new territory, and it is an evolving process. We are just getting to a point where established organizations that set standards, like APA Style, the MLA Style Manual, and the Chicago Manual of Style, are addressing the challenges of citations with AI tools. It's likely that we feel uncomfortable or disagree with the way forward, especially as each educator is grappling with these new tools and their impact on writing instruction across content areas.

In fact, the seismic shift of writing with AI tools (with all of their possibilities and potential problems) can be compared to the worldwide transition from oral history and memorization to writing in ancient times, the shift from handwriting on scrolls to the printing press in the Renaissance era, or the progression from printed books, articles, and journals to e-books and digital texts in the last decade of the twentieth century.

Yeah, it's that big.

This is a radical paradigm change from the way our educational undergraduate courses taught future teachers or second-career educators in graduate programs. Quite obviously, it'll take time for the world of education to reset, adjust, and become more standardized. AI-supported writing is new to everyone, so it will take a while to transition to AI-ready educators.

Here are six ways (also adapted from Dr. Eaton's work) that you can view the current debates on writing in the post-AI world and put them in context:

1. **Hybrid Writing:** Where Human and AI Intellect Collide: Integrating human and AI writing means pioneering new creative frontiers. As

the boundaries blur, there's a unique space where human intellect coexists with AI input. Educators must cultivate creativity and teach responsible AI use.

2. **AI-Enhanced Creativity:** A Catalyst for Imagination: AI augments rather than replaces human creativity. As an imaginative catalyst, AI sparks thinking and pushes creative boundaries. Students achieve new creative heights by learning to harness AI thoughtfully and ethically.

3. **Transcending Language Barriers:** AI Bridges Language Divides: Generative AI breakthroughs in language translation herald a future where language barriers could become a thing of the past. AI translation enables a universal translator, promoting inclusivity and global connections. A caveat, though: AI must respect cultural nuance, and educators must ensure its responsible use.

4. **With Great AI Comes Great Responsibility:** Why Ethics Matter: While AI aids writing, all of us remain responsible for the ideas we write and, as importantly, teach students to write. As critical thinkers, our role is now even more crucial. We must validate AI's accuracy and ensure its ethical use. Bottom line: Students must learn to write responsibly with AI.

5. **Attribution in the Age of Algorithms:** Giving Credit Still Counts: Even with AI's help, citations matter. Attribution reminds us of shared knowledge and is a habit to instill in students. Citing AI tools and the sources that inform them are key to transparency.

6. **Rethinking Plagiarism:** Finding Nuance in the AI Era: AI co-creation requires rethinking plagiarism policies, not rewriting them. Educators must revise policies to suit this hybrid era fairly. This includes teaching students to use AI tools transparently, paraphrase the AI content, and use the correct citation formats.

PENETRATING THE JUNGLE OF PLAGIARISM, CHEATING, AND ACADEMIC INTEGRITY IN AN AI WORLD

AI writing tools and chatbots like ChatGPT, Google Gemini, Claude, and Microsoft Copilot compel us to reexamine concepts like "cheating" and "plagiarism" in a new light. The first step, though, is to reassess how we teach writing and provide feedback.

While today's technology will seem primitive in years to come, the aim of education remains unchanged: to cultivate creativity, critical thinking, and communication in all our students' academic pursuits. As long as students demonstrate these through their work—whether achieved through human effort alone or as a collaboration between human and AI tools—we can still measure if growth and learning have occurred.

Let's look at some of these scenarios inspired by a *Ditch That Textbook* blog post (Miller, 2022) about AI and plagiarism:

- A student uses an AI writing assistant to help brainstorm ideas and organize his thoughts. The student then leverages these to draft an essay in his own words and based on his understanding, submitting the final work for feedback. (Permissible)
- A student has an AI tool evaluate a draft essay and suggest improvements to better articulate key themes. She considers each suggestion, accepting some and revising the essay to submit based on her learning and goals for the assignment. (Permissible)
- A student copies and pastes large sections from an AI-generated essay with little understanding or further elaboration. (Not Permissible)

Try to see AI as a tool to spark creativity and teach writing incrementally with checkpoints and regular feedback while—at the same time—teaching students how to transparently and thoughtfully use these tools to improve their writing and communication.

Fluency in leveraging AI effectively and judiciously is an essential skill your students need both now and in their future careers. Rather than setting rigid rules that may disadvantage students, educators need guidelines on how to amplify student learning by collaborating with AI at different levels. The key is to cultivate student competency in applying AI responsibly to achieve their goals and gain new insights. With educational policies and teaching assignments designed around this collaboration, students can partner with AI to enhance their capabilities.

Personal values are at the heart of our human-centered pedagogy. Education is about developing people and citizens as much as skills. While we don't need to have answers today, we must pursue them with humanity in mind and a view of AI as an instrument to uplift us and make our world better. By empowering students and educators to demystify generative AI tools and learn how to leverage them ethically and transparently, we create the potential for humans and machines to forge a better future where technology inspires our human-ness rather than defines it.

What's So Great about Instructional and Generative AI Tools, and How Can I Use Them?

Great questions! Let's scout the world of AI and clear up the murkiness around instructional AI and generative AI. These two sets of AI tools serve different purposes and are both game-changers in the educational landscape.

Instructional AI is your go-to for anything directly related to teaching and learning. Generative AI, while not tailor-made for the classroom, has a broader range of talents and can still bring its A-game to educational settings.

DIGGING INTO INSTRUCTIONAL AI TOOLS

Instructional AI is your classroom superhero, custom-tailored to bolster teaching and learning. Imagine a teaching assistant who is constantly available and adjusts to the individual preferences and learning styles of each student. The goal is to supercharge educational outcomes, making learning more effective and your life as an educator a bit easier:

- **Personalized Learning:** Think of it as your class turned into a personalized learning playground. Every student gets more support for their lessons, such as adjusted reading levels or vocabulary support, that is tuned to their own pace and interests.
- **Task Automation:** Grading assignments during family movie night? Nope. Instructional AI takes care of the admin grind, freeing you up to engage with your students and (bonus!) your own family.
- **Smart Content Creation:** Need a killer lesson plan? This AI crafts educational materials that resonate with each student, giving you an edge in the classroom.

Basically, when you leverage instructional AI at its best, it focuses on student learning, lesson improvement, and community building.

One great example of instructional AI is **Packback**. It's like a writing coach in the digital world. Think of it as a supportive community for students, where they submit their writing and get immediate, personalized feedback. It's not just a cold algorithm talking back to them; it's a tool that understands their unique writing style and needs. Plus, students connect with peers, share insights, and grow together.

Other platforms that leverage instructional AI in writing include **Turnitin**, **Grammarly**, and **Writable**. Each of these tools is explicitly designed to guide student writing with the help of AI feedback.

Another example is **Khanmigo** by Khan Academy. It's a broader instructional AI tool that focuses on more than just writing. It does support student writing, but it also extends its helping hand to students in science, social studies, and math. This guides students with follow-up prompts and questions without giving the answers. It provides sentence ideas and starters but not a complete essay. It is intended to be an assistant for students as they go through the learning process, not just a tool that gives them the answers.

SchoolAI is a writing tool and so much more; it champions the individual learning journey of each student by providing personalized, one-on-one tutoring, guidance, and support. This tailored approach ensures that all learners receive the attention and resources they need to succeed based on their unique needs and learning pace. The platform enables educators to craft specific "Spaces" (learning environments) equipped with personalized instructions and content. This feature allows for a more adaptable and responsive teaching approach, where learning experiences can be customized to fit the diverse needs of a classroom. Also, SchoolAI integrates AI-powered chatbots capable of embodying historical figures or serving as learning assistants. These chatbots offer students an engaging and interactive educational experience, making learning more dynamic and accessible.

Class Companion is an AI teaching assistant tool that provides instant, personalized feedback on written assignments, enhancing students' learning experience. It allows for self-paced learning with features for practicing, receiving feedback, and making revisions. Teachers can use their own rubrics or preloaded rubrics to provide students with instant feedback on their writing. The tool is versatile, suitable for various subjects, and free for both teachers and students.

Magic School AI is a platform that aids teachers in creating educational content, generating assignments, and catering to diverse classroom needs. It includes a rubric generator, IEP creator, and text leveler (among other tools) to streamline content creation and paperwork. Magic School AI also uses generative AI for tasks like proofreading and summarizing text. It's a

AI GOES TO SCHOOL

free service that offers insights into student learning patterns, saving teachers time and enhancing their efficiency.

Brisk Teaching is another AI tool and Chrome extension that has a simple set of tools to generate ideas and writing supports. It also provides feedback, inspects writing to make sure it is student-created and not prompted with AI, and adjusts the reading levels of the texts you select as the teacher to help you differentiate for your students. It's simple to use and easy to implement with the approval of your IT team and school- or district-level leadership.

More examples of instructive AI are showing up every day to help educators with the unique challenges of K–12 education. The shift from generative AI to instructive AI is a necessary transition so that with these tools, we can maintain academic integrity, provide our students with personalized support, and save time.

FOLLOWING UP WITH GENERATIVE AI TOOLS

Generative AI, on the other hand, is like your creative buddy who's good at just about everything. It has limitless possibilities and assists you with text, data, images, videos, and computer coding support, as well as being able to analyze all those modes. It's your creative partner, teaching assistant, grading support, differentiation expert, sentence stem creator, translator ... and the list keeps going. For teachers, it's the just-in-time backup and support you need to free you up to build on those personal relationships with your students.

Exploring the integration of artificial intelligence tools like OpenAI's ChatGPT, Google's Gemini, Microsoft Copilot, and Anthropic's Claude helps educators transform their lessons, assessments, and other components of teaching and learning to personalize their students' experiences ... as long as they take the time to know their students well. These generative AI technologies refine and enrich the student learning journey across multiple dimensions, such as crafting personalized learning experiences, facilitating research projects, bolstering review and assessment mechanisms, and enriching vocabulary and translation capabilities.

The integration of generative AI in education is transforming the nuts and bolts of lesson planning, content creation, writing assignments, and the overall approach to teaching and learning. This leap forward is opening up a treasure trove of possibilities, making the educational journey richer for both teachers and students.

122

- **Lesson Planning:** It's like having a magic wand for lesson preparation. Generative AI whips up a variety of educational resources—from assessment questions and learning goals to activities that push students to think more deeply. It's clever enough to suggest lesson ideas and tweak activities to fit the diverse mix of learners in a classroom, ensuring every lesson is well-rounded and flexible.
- **Writing Tasks:** Here, AI tools are your sidekicks, handling the nitty-gritty of admin and communication. Imagine automating the drafting of emails to parents, crafting recommendation letters, or even creating permission slips for outings. Beyond admin, these tools also spin social stories that support social-emotional learning and offer tailored feedback on student work, making learning more personalized.
- **Instructional Design and Delivery:** Generative AI is breaking new ground here by making lessons more inclusive and tailored to various learning needs. It adapts lesson plans with different teaching strategies, draws up detailed agendas, and spotlights essential terms, enriching the educational content. Plus, incorporating teacher-approved AI-generated materials into lessons brings a fresh and interactive dimension to learning and aligns technology with educational objectives.

In the evolving landscape of education, generative AI emerges as an empowering force, redefining personalization, accessibility, and the role of educators. With its ability to analyze vast amounts of student data—while adhering to stringent privacy standards—AI crafts personalized learning pathways that dynamically adjust to each student's proficiency level, suggesting tailored resources and modulating question difficulty to optimize learning experiences. Beyond mere content delivery, generative AI, embodied in chatbots, serves as an always-on tutor, offering round-the-clock assistance, diverse explanations, and instantaneous feedback, thereby fostering an environment where learning never ceases.

The creative capacity of AI extends into content generation, empowering educators to transcend traditional material preparation. By automating the creation of lesson outlines, example problems, and writing prompts, AI enables teachers to concentrate on more specific, student-centered instructional strategies and spend more time building student relationships. Moreover, AI's ever-improving translation tools offer support for English Language Learners, and soon, the tools will reduce or remove language barriers and facilitate a more inclusive educational setting.

Yet this brave new world of generative AI in education isn't without its quandaries. The ghost of plagiarism is ever-present, urging the adoption of sophisticated detection tools and a solid ethical framework to uphold academic honesty. And while AI might mimic understanding, it falls short of fostering the nuanced critical thinking and deep knowledge that are the hallmarks of effective education. Teachers control the wheel, steering students to question AI-generated content critically and sift through it for accuracy, especially when faced with AI's occasional drift into the realm of the inaccurate or misleading.

Looking ahead, the potential of generative AI in education is boundless. Future developments could include AI-generated interactive simulations tailored to individual learning objectives, adaptive tools that modify their approach based on a student's emotional state to enhance engagement, and collaborative efforts between AI and educators to conceive novel assessment methods transcending conventional testing paradigms. This new era of education, powered by generative AI, promises a landscape where personalized learning, accessibility, and the enrichment of teaching methodologies coalesce to herald an unprecedented revolution in how education is delivered and experienced.

Generative AI tools are not classroom-specific; rather, they offer applications such as:

- **Content Generation:** Whether it's penning a blog or creating a digital art masterpiece, generative AI has the creative skills.
- **Algorithm Creation:** It can dream up new machine learning algorithms—yes, an AI creating other AIs. Mind-blowing, right?

WRAPPING IT UP

What's the main lesson here? It's that instructional AI is laser-focused on pedagogy and the development of each individual student. It is designed from the ground up to improve teaching and learning. However, generative AI is the Swiss Army knife of the AI industry.

Here's another analogy:

Imagine you're at a crossroads where two paths diverge: one leads to a classroom and the other leads to an artist's studio. That's the difference between instructional AI and generative AI.

- **Instructional AI:** This is the path to the classroom. It's all about teaching and learning. The AI acts like a tutor, understanding each student's needs and helping them grow. It's the personal touch, the tailored advice, the gentle nudge in the right direction. It's turning technology into a compassionate educator.
- **Generative AI:** Now head to the artist's studio. Here, AI is the creator, the inventor, the imaginative mind. It's not interested in teaching but in crafting something new, like text, images, or music. It's a broad brush, painting with data and algorithms to produce content that's indistinguishable from human-made art.

Table 6.1 shows a more visual way to understand the differences:

Feature	Instructional AI	Generative AI
Purpose	To help students learn	To create new content
Focus	On individual students	On the general population
Feedback	Personalized	Generic
Goal	To improve student learning	To mimic human creativity

Table 6.1: Comparing Instructional and Generative AI Tools.

Instructional AI helps students bloom through nurturing and growth. Generative AI, on the other hand, is the artistic creator, inventing and innovating. When you combine them thoughtfully as part of your teaching and learning process, they level up your teaching and improve student learning. They are two paths, each with its unique use and purpose, guiding us toward a more enriched educational landscape that heightens a human-centered education when combined with great pedagogy and thoughtful, critical educators.

HOW DO I CHECK FOR PLAGIARISM?

Navigating the world of plagiarism checkers in education is akin to walking a tightrope, where the balance between their benefits and pitfalls requires careful consideration. These tools play a pivotal role in upholding academic integrity and encouraging the originality that's vital for student growth. Yet, it's essential to peel back the layers to understand their broader impact, including their limitations and the biases they may harbor. In the intricate dance with plagiarism detection tools like **ZeroGPT** and others, striking the right balance is key.

Pros of Plagiarism Checkers

- **Fosters Originality:** These digital sentinels stand guard against a copy-paste culture, nudging your students to develop their unique voices and insights. Encouraging originality is a cornerstone of intellectual maturity.
- **Spotlights Unintentional Plagiarism:** It's not uncommon for students to echo existing ideas unknowingly. Plagiarism checkers shed light on these moments, turning them into teachable instances to master the art of citation and thus elevate their scholarly craft.
- **Sharpens Research Skills:** The act of dissecting flagged sections by these tools can fine-tune your students' research prowess, enriching their understanding of academic integrity.
- **Empowers Educators:** By shouldering the burden of an initial plagiarism screening, these tools carve out more space for teachers to focus on personalized feedback and instruction.

Cons of Plagiarism Checkers

- **Overdependence Hazard:** There's a looming risk that reliance on these tools might eclipse the nurturing of core research and critical thinking skills.
- **Quantitative Score Trap:** The allure of low plagiarism scores might be misleading, as true academic brilliance lies in the substance, not just originality metrics.
- **Creative Dampening:** Overzealous plagiarism policing could deter students from weaving a rich tapestry of sources into their work, fearing undue penalization.

Bias and Fairness Concerns

- **Western Bias:** The tilt toward Western-centric databases can unfairly disadvantage non-Western citations, mistaking them for plagiarism.
- **Ingrained Algorithmic Biases:** The very algorithms that power these tools may reflect the biases of their training data, potentially skewing flags against marginalized voices.

Navigating Toward Fairness and Integrity

- **Teacher Awareness:** Educators must stay alert to these tools' biases, applying a critical eye to their findings.
- **Encouragement of Diverse Sources:** Motivate students to draw from a wide array of reputable sources, enriching their work with varied global insights.
- **Critical Source Evaluation Focus:** Teaching should underscore the importance of critically vetting sources, going beyond what plagiarism checkers suggest.

Can I Use AI for Reliable Assessments?

Yes ... and no. Let's cover the main points.

INCORPORATING AI INTO VALID ASSESSMENTS

AI tools are invaluable for providing formative feedback. What if students could shape their own learning path? Imagine a classroom where AI helps students by providing valuable information to identify strengths and weaknesses. By providing personalized feedback, AI guides students to refine their approach. Teachers still orchestrate the assessments, but there are purposeful and inclusive parts of the project or writing where you thoughtfully incorporate generative AI tools to help students get feedback throughout the process.

Ideally, teachers combine AI and human judgment to ensure a more rounded and accurate evaluation, especially for complex assessments. AI analyzes data and detects patterns in ways educators might miss. But remember that AI is just a tool. Grading is still a human endeavor. To ensure validity, fairness, and reliability, you need to closely monitor AI-based assessments, adjusting as necessary.

Here are examples of how you can use AI tools for student assessments:

- Use Class Companion to provide real-time support for students' writing based on pre-created rubric templates (if your school and IT department have approved them) or your own school or district rubric.
- If you're helping your students prepare for a Socratic Seminar, provide specific instructions to SchoolAI's chatbot about what you are discussing. It can assist students in understanding the other side's arguments by creating a session and having students join virtually, similar to Nearpod or Blooket.
- You can even use Byte, by CodeBreakerEdu, an interface that accesses a chatbot powered by ChatGPT 3.5 Turbo. You don't have to create an account or exchange any personally identifiable information, making it safe, no matter what the student data privacy laws are in your state or country. This tool does not require student accounts, so it's even more useful.
- If you are having students research a specific person, assign School AI's Character bot to your class using the same process, but use a pseudonym or class number. You minimize the personally identifiable information since no student accounts are necessary.

All these ideas take approval and coordination with your administration and IT departments but can be extremely helpful. Remember, though, that AI cannot replace the nuances of human grading, especially in high-stakes assessments. AI struggles with evaluating higher-order thinking skills such as critical thinking, creativity, and problem-solving, which are essential components of many assignments.

For the valid integration of AI in student assessment, the key is to be transparent. Make sure everyone is aware of how you'll use AI in skills assessments. To expect ethical, honest, and transparent AI use from students requires that you, as their teacher, model these ideals. This includes informing students, parents, community members, school board members, school and district administrators, and other stakeholders. The more explicit and honest you are with *when* and *how* you use these AI tools, the better you'll be at helping students understand how to use them effectively and transparently.

ENGAGING STUDENTS TO SET LEARNING GOALS

For meaningful learning, students need to be active participants in the process. Encourage them to determine their own assessment goals and criteria, deciding on the appropriate balance between AI and human roles in the assessment process. AI provides invaluable formative feedback, helping students to continuously improve. Still, as mentioned before, complex assessments should primarily reflect human evaluation that considers aspects AI may overlook.

Transparency is crucial here. Address your students' concerns about AI tools and explain how they're being used in the learning process. You and your students can analyze which types of assessment would benefit from AI versus human judgment, considering factors such as the nature of the assignment, the learning objectives, and their personal learning styles. Educators can use the tools listed previously, such as **Brisk Teaching** and **SchoolAI**, to help with the process of feedback.

GRADING TASK SUBCOMPONENTS

As we are all aware, grading is multilayered and consists of much more than just assigning a letter grade. Distributed assessment, where each subcomponent of a task is graded, encourages students to view assignments as an entire learning journey rather than just a final product.

Feedback is the driving force of learning, truly coming alive when it's woven throughout the journey, not just at the end. Picture this: a learning journey where each step is an opportunity for growth, with AI playing the role of a nurturing guide alongside the wisdom of educators. It's like having a personal coach who provides gentle nudges toward excellence, ensuring no opportunity for improvement is missed. Together, educators and AI create a powerful alliance, offering feedback that's not only timely but deeply tailored to each student's needs. This collaboration sets the stage for a rich learning experience where growth is continuous and every learner finds their path to shine.

Incorporating AI tools into the creation of a five-paragraph essay could unfold as follows:

- First, leverage AI to craft a table of contents or a compelling starting sentence, marking these early steps in the assessment checkpoints. This initial engagement with AI sets the tone for a structured and thoughtful approach to essay writing. Then, as students complete their first draft, it becomes another crucial checkpoint, where the educator's insights provide the first layer of refinement.

- Following this, the spotlight turns back to AI, offering students a chance to receive and integrate feedback on their draft. This step, meticulously recorded in the milestone checkpoint, ensures students are engaging with AI's constructive advice.
- Next, peer editing introduces a collaborative dimension, enriching the revision process with diverse perspectives.
- Finally, students refine their essays with peer suggestions, culminating in the submission of their work for a comprehensive evaluation.

This structured approach enhances the essay's quality and deepens students' engagement with the writing process.

Generative AI helps the strategy of requiring draft submissions to shine. It allows for a closer examination of students' evolving work and the opportunity to steer them toward ethical AI use. AI's capability to provide instant, bespoke feedback acts as a deterrent against plagiarism, promoting a culture of originality and self-assessment.

This approach enables educators to track the progression of students' assignments from ideation to execution, providing them with a more comprehensive understanding of each student's learning journey. AI captures a student's entire process from "Eureka!" to completion.

Emphasizing active learning and promoting self-improvement, AI tools provide real-time feedback on each stage of an assignment. This allows students to make necessary adjustments and improvements along the way, encouraging reflexivity and iterative learning.

MOVING TO MORE AUTHENTIC ASSESSMENTS

To provide a more comprehensive evaluation of student learning, consider implementing alternative assessment formats and including performance elements. Let's review our current toolbox of assessments and break free from the mold of traditional tests and quizzes.

Let's make assessments that reflect the real world, not just the classroom. Authentic assessments evaluate real-world skills. AI customizes these for each student, ensuring fair assessments with the same criteria. Students connect with relatable assessments, and outcomes genuinely reflect abilities. Socratic Seminars are great ways to measure student understanding since

> Let's make assessments go beyond check-the-box exercises and become holistic showcases of student prowess.

students do not have screens in front of them during the discussion.

It's time to embrace a palette of evaluation methods that better capture the full spectrum of your students' abilities. Think portfolio assessments, think project-based evaluations, think real-world problem-solving tasks. Why stop at having students fill in the blanks when they can demonstrate their understanding through performance elements?

Imagine a history class where students don't just write about the Civil Rights Movement but also create a multimedia presentation or stage a mini-drama. This is education coming to life! By incorporating these alternative formats and performance elements, we're assessing while engaging, challenging, and—most importantly—empowering our students to show what they're truly capable of. Let's make assessments go beyond check-the-box exercises and become holistic showcases of student prowess.

AI tools support these formats, such as by providing feedback on clarity in a video presentation or by suggesting improvements to an artistic representation based on aesthetic principles.

No matter the format, make sure your students understand what you expect from them. Assess all formats using equitable criteria and provide constructive feedback for improvement. Incorporating AI tools into alternative assessments enhances each learning experience while maintaining the focus on students' understanding and skills.

REBOOT

Educators must maintain a delicate equilibrium between the benefits of using AI tools, academic integrity policies, and the issues that arise with rampant plagiarism.

Consider one Illinois school district that, in its recent quest to combat AI plagiarism, decided to block useful websites like Quill. This platform assisted students with paraphrasing and provided feedback on their language mistakes. Numerous high school students confided to their teachers about the hardships they faced as a result since they relied on such platforms to provide support with their writing. Often, they used it to overcome language barriers if English was a second language or if they did not have the academic background knowledge to help provide guidance and support with their writing or homework.

We can either choose to turn a blind eye or step up, lead the discussion, and guide our students and schools through these transformative times. As mentioned earlier in this chapter, Dr. Eaton's insightful tenets on plagiarism provide a valuable roadmap for our AI journey, altering our perspectives on creativity, language, responsibility, attribution, and plagiarism (Eaton, 2023). We benefit our learners if we embrace this expedition with a spirit of curiosity while placing human intellect and imagination in the lead.

This new era of co-creation with AI isn't merely a shift; it's an exhilarating transformation. By nurturing our students' creativity and ethical grounding, we can make the most of this change. Please join the conversation in your educational circles, sharing your insights on the role of AI in schools and discussing how we can use it to create a positive influence in our learning environments.

Together, let's craft a bright future where technology amplifies our shared human potential.

Part III
Navigating the Emerging Opportunities and Challenges of AI in Education

Perhaps we should all stop for a moment and focus not only on making our AI better and more successful but also on the benefit of humanity.

— *Stephen Hawking, theoretical physicist and cosmologist*

Image P3: Let's work together and discuss the future of AI's role in learning.

Chapter 7
Embracing AI-Created Art

The tools and technologies we've developed are really the first few drops of water in the vast ocean of what AI can do.

— Fei-Fei Li, American computer scientist and AI researcher

Image 7.1: AI art—embracing the palette of bytes and brushstrokes.

J oin me as we take up a virtual brush and paint a vivid tableau where technology and creativity become a seamless blend of human imagination and artificial vision. Welcome to the captivating world of AI-generated art, a world that opens new horizons for learning, creativity, and the future.

Our intriguing journey began over half a century ago. In the mid-twentieth century, pioneers of algorithmic art began to experiment with the fusion of algorithms and artistic expression, creating a powerful synergy that hinted at the vast creative potential of technology. One such pioneer, painter Harold Cohen, developed AI capable of autonomously producing abstract paintings with a consistent artistic style, which Harold called AARON. These early efforts, albeit limited, were instrumental in shaping future AI artists and their creators.

Fast-forward a few decades to the 1990s, and we encounter the emergence of style transfer techniques. This development allowed AI to emulate the styles of renowned artists, thereby imparting a touch of the familiar to otherwise uncharted territory. By 2006, with the advent of neural networks, AI began to generate psychedelic and surreal images, beautifully demonstrating the imaginative capabilities of these machine learning models.

The AI art narrative took a revolutionary turn in 2014 when Ian Goodfellow and his colleagues introduced Generative Adversarial Networks (GANs). GANs represent an intricate ballet of two neural networks: the Generator (the creative spirit producing new data instances) and the Discriminator (the critical eye evaluating these creations). Through a dynamic of competition and collaboration, these networks achieve truly awe-inspiring results.

In 2015, Google's DeepDream, utilizing GANs, offered a striking illustration of this teamwork by transforming ordinary images into dream-like landscapes, flexing the imaginative muscle of AI. However, the seminal moment that propelled AI art into mainstream consciousness came in 2018 when the *Portrait of Edmond de Belamy*, an AI-generated portrait created by Obvious using a GAN, fetched $432,500 at a Christie's auction. This event signaled the acceptance of AI-generated art into the hallowed halls of the traditional art world.

In our contemporary era, AI is intricately shaping our relationship with creativity, stimulating discussions about its role in society while enhancing daily life. Our homes and classrooms are transforming into dynamic canvases of creation, serving as laboratories where human ingenuity and AI intertwine. For educators like us, AI-generated art presents a unique opportunity to innovate pedagogically, promoting critical and creative thinking, fostering digital literacy, and reimagining curricula through the fusion of art and AI.

The aim here is not to replace human art but to magnify it, to use AI as a tool for broadening our creative horizons and pushing the boundaries of the possible. By blending art and AI, we can inspire innovation, nurture digital fluency, and inject a fresh wave of creativity into our curricula. Far from overshadowing the human touch, AI serves to enhance it, making the process of learning even more vibrant and engaging.

So, are you ready to invite this artistic revolution into your classroom? Are you prepared to embrace the potential of AI art as a catalyst for educational transformation? If so, let's embark on this thrilling adventure together. In our journey, algorithms and code, pixels and creativity become inseparable components of the human story that continues to be written. Our journey begins here, but where it will lead remains a vibrant canvas, waiting for our collective imagination to bring it to life.

How Does AI-Generated Art Support My Teaching?

Ever wonder, "What's the deal with AI and art? Can it actually apply to my classroom?" Let's dive in and find out.

Imagine creating a unique image to help English learners master a specific vocabulary word. You likely use visual literary strategies, whether they're focused on English learners or your entire class.

Now consider accomplishing this in moments by prompting an AI tool instead of searching online endlessly. An image is created not with a brush but with lines of code. These are not just robotic stick figures, right? Not even close! AI-generated art is powered by a special type of machine learning called GANs, mentioned earlier in this chapter.

Let's demystify GANs a bit more with a simple metaphor: envision an artist and a critic in a creative dance. The artist paints, the critic critiques, and so the cycle goes, culminating in something remarkably close to human-generated art. Those are GANs for you! In fact, I created every image in this book with the help of AI to demonstrate the possibilities while covering the ethical and moral dilemmas that exist with this technology.

BROADENING THE EDUCATIONAL CANVAS

Here are a few teacher-centered ways that AI-generated art engages learning, even without students creating it on their own. *NOTE:* Many students may already have versions of these apps on their smartphones, using them for entertainment instead of learning.

- **Storytelling:** Visual Aids for English Learners: Think of yourself as an educator and a visual storyteller. When you're teaching academic vocabulary to English learners, imagine using AI to generate images that precisely illustrate the concept at hand. For example, instead of a generic picture of an ecosystem, what if you could present a vivid, custom-made image of a coral reef? This personalization is often a game-changer for ELs.

> Beyond the sheer cool factor, AI-generated art opens up an expansive universe of creative possibilities.

- **The General Classroom:** Cultivate Critical Thinking: Picture your social studies class studying democracy. An AI tool generates contrasting images that symbolize different governance systems. These visuals serve as catalysts for deeper understanding and critical discussions.
- **Math and Sciences:** Abstract No More: For math and science educators, AI-generated art is your secret weapon. What if you could teach the Pythagorean theorem with an AI-generated, dynamic, step-by-step visual guide that makes abstract concepts become real?
- **Literature and Humanities:** Bring Texts to Life: In the humanities, how about using AI-generated art to visualize the settings or characters in *To Kill a Mockingbird*? You're not just teaching a book ... you're creating an immersive experience.
- **Special Education:** Tailored Teaching Tools: Special ed teachers, meet your new best friend. Imagine having the ability to design customized visuals tailored to diverse learning needs. For a child with autism, for example, you can generate sensory-friendly yet educational images.

- **Interdisciplinary Learning:** The World Is Your Canvas: Why not create interdisciplinary lesson plans using AI-generated art? A lesson that combines science and art to explore the geometry in famous artworks is a concept your students may never forget.

By embracing AI-generated art, you're adopting new technology and expanding how you teach. Make your classroom a gallery of the future, where every pixel serves not just to please the eye but to enlighten the mind.

UNDERSTANDING WHY AI-GENERATED ART MATTERS

You might ask, "Why should I care about AI in art?" Beyond the sheer cool factor, AI-generated art opens up an expansive universe of creative possibilities. It welcomes students to the captivating intersection of tech and art, ignites innovation, and promotes collaboration. Plus, it offers a new, engaging way to equip students with essential digital skills through a creative lens.

Intrigued? Let's talk about how you can bring this tech-powered artistic revolution right into your classroom.

AI art tools offer an engaging way to cultivate students' understanding of AI and machine learning. Imagine students playing the role of Picasso, creating unique pieces with AI while learning how algorithms work behind the scenes. Hands-on experience with these technologies promotes critical thinking, creative problem-solving, and digital literacy.

NOTE: As we discussed in Chapter 3, please refer to your school and district curriculum and IT leaders and check educational policies before you introduce this to students. Make sure you are aligned with student data privacy laws and policies, and, if needed, reach out to your students' families before you use AI art-generation tools.

Now, on to the fun stuff …

While it's an enjoyable, creative exploration, AI art education also develops valuable digital skills and ways of thinking that serve students well beyond a single project. By creating cutting-edge tools, they gain a sense of empowerment as well as a sense of responsibility for how they build and apply those tools. AI becomes a means for students to find and share their unique voices to positively impact the world.

Benefits of using AI art tools include:

- **Learning AI and machine learning fundamentals in a fun, creative context:** Students discover how algorithms analyze data to generate new images, videos, music, and more. This demystifies AI and builds technical skills for the future.
- **Developing creativity through experimentation:** Open-ended AI art projects give students the freedom to explore their interests and talents. They can try different styles, subjects, and mediums to push creative boundaries.
- **Improving problem-solving through troubleshooting:** Working with AI systems challenges students to overcome obstacles, whether fixing a bug in their code or refining a prompt to achieve their desired artistic vision. Best of all, students learn perseverance and resilience.
- **Cultivating an inquisitive mindset:** Coming up with thought-provoking prompts or what if questions to generate art expands imagination and curiosity about the world. Students develop an ability to ask deeper, more nuanced questions about themselves, others, and the role of technology.
- **Learning responsible innovation:** Creating AI art raises ethical questions about the appropriate use of technology and bias in data and algorithms. In addition, discussing challenges and using AI to benefit others fosters social awareness and ethical reasoning.

With guidance, our students become creators, not just consumers, of technology. They gain digital fluency through hands-on human experiences enhanced by AI. These creative AI adventures cultivate humanity in a digital age and help students reach their full potential as independent thinkers and tech-savvy visionaries. See Image 7.2.

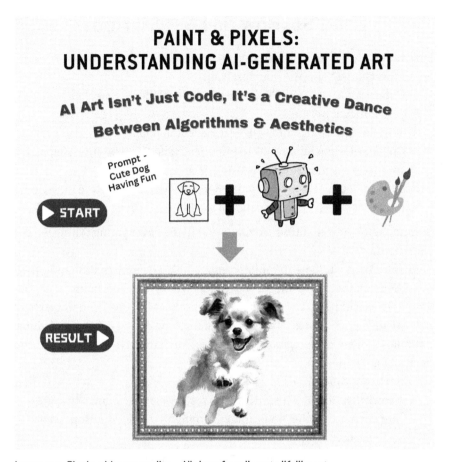

Image 7.2: Pixels with personality—AI's leap from lines to lifelike art.

Cool! So, How Do I Get Started?

First, here's a quick list of first steps you can take in the AI-generated art world.

A Mini-Guide: Your AI Art Action Plan:

- **Choose an AI Art Tool:** Pick a user-friendly platform that aligns with your educational goals.
- **Start Small:** Test the tool with a single lesson plan.
- **Collaborate and Share:** Talk to other teachers. You'll be surprised at the creative ways they're already using AI-generated art.
- **Stay Updated:** AI evolves rapidly. Keep an eye out for new features and tools that enrich your educational toolkit.

Second, here's how to introduce this world to the eager young minds in your classroom.

Inspire your students to embark on creative adventures designing their own AI-generated art projects. Encourage them to experiment with different styles, subjects, and forms of expression. AI opens up a universe of new creative possibilities, allowing students to push beyond the traditional boundaries of art. Even regularly used tools like Canva give users an option to create AI-generated art.

Ideas to get you started:

- A work inspired by a historical event or social issue about which they care deeply. Creating art around meaningful themes develops passion and purpose.
- A piece reflecting their unique personal vision or style. AI gives them the freedom to explore what most interests or inspires them as individuals.
- A whimsical mashup of unexpected styles, subjects, and mediums. The joy of AI is discovering what emerges from unusual combinations, just like in human imagination.
- An interactive art experience that comes alive for the viewer. Students can make AI-generated art that responds and changes based on someone engaging with their creation.

The possibilities are truly endless with AI, limited only by your students' curiosity and enthusiasm. AI-generated art allows them to develop technical skills while following their passions, gain exposure to new art forms, and build creative confidence through experimentation. While AI may be the

With guidance, our students become creators, not just consumers, of technology.

tool, students remain the artists. The projects are meaningful and memorable because learners are crafting something imaginative and revealing about themselves and how they use this technology.

Overall, this AI-powered adventure cultivates valuable life skills that will serve students well beyond a single classroom project. An openness to new ideas, courage to take creative risks, and the ability to use technology to express individuality are all critical for success in an increasingly complex world. The future is made by dreamers, inventors, and artists. AI-generated art helps students become all three.

The key is to strike a balance between structure and openness. Provide guidance and examples to inspire, then give students the freedom to explore where their curiosity leads. The results may surprise and delight you. Your students may discover new talents and interests that neither you nor they knew they possessed. AI helps ignite their creative spark.

ENCOURAGING TEAMWORK TO MAKE THE DREAM WORK

Foster teamwork in AI-powered art projects, a move that sharpens problem-solving, critical thinking, and people skills. Collaboration creates a dynamic platform for sharing ideas and perspectives, fostering innovative and creative solutions.

By encouraging teamwork in AI-generated art projects, you can help students develop the soft skills as well as the tech skills they need to be successful in school and beyond.

BLENDING ART AND CODING

Integrating art and coding builds a foundation for a solid STEAM education. Students learn programming and logic to develop AI artist tools and create their works of art. Such interdisciplinary approaches spark a passion for learning and build versatile thinking skills.

Benefits of fusing art and code include:

- **Developing Computational Thinking:** Building an AI art system challenges students to logically analyze a problem, break it into basic steps, troubleshoot issues, and achieve creative goals. They gain invaluable experience translating human intuitions and abilities into code.

- **Learning in an Engaging Way:** Creating their own AI artists or using platforms where they can customize machine learning models to generate art brings coding to life and taps into student passions and interests. Abstract concepts become concrete through hands-on experimentation and personal artwork.

- **Seeing Connections across Disciplines:** Combining art and code shows students how skills in one area apply to another, and that real-world challenges often require hybrid thinking across STEAM subjects. They start to connect the dots between various fields, developing more flexible and broadly capable mindsets.

- **Solving Open-Ended Problems:** AI art projects have no single right answer, giving students opportunities to determine the problems they want to solve and the best ways of addressing them. This cultivates determination, imagination, and design-thinking abilities.

- **Building Valuable Technical and Life Skills:** Coding AI art equips students with skills that are essential for innovation in the twenty-first century. Even more so, it gives them confidence in using technology to explore and express individuality. Students discover they have both the creative vision and the power to shape the tools of tomorrow.

Let's foster renaissance learners who see beyond the boundaries of past disciplines or divisions. Creativity amplified by technology is the future, and AI art fusing imagination and logic cultivates talent our future leaders urgently need. Your students build the world their art inhabits. With code, they craft the tools for crafting that world. Art meets engineering, and students reach their full potential at the intersection.

DISCUSSING, REFLECTING, AND LEARNING

Meaningful classroom discussions about AI and human-made art develop your students' critical thinking skills and their understanding of technology's role in creativity. Comparing differences and similarities between the two art forms leads to insights into their relationship and impact on the world.

Discussion points might include:

Differences

- AI art is generated by algorithms and data, while human art comes from imagination and emotion. What is lost or gained with each approach?
- AI art can be produced rapidly, but human art takes time. Does speed always mean less thoughtfulness or value? When does it enhance or diminish creativity?
- AI art may achieve photorealism, but human art is abstract. Are they mutually exclusive or complementary forms of expression?

Similarities

- Both AI and human art can be appreciated for beauty, emotion, vision, and capturing truth. What makes us see the humanity or "heart" in each form of art?
- Art communicates ideas, inspires contemplation, and binds us together in shared experiences. In what ways does art created by artificial or human intelligence build connections across cultures and generations?

These rich discussions develop empathy, ethics, and higher-order reasoning. Students may debate whether AI art qualifies as *real* art and its power for both propaganda and greater inclusion. They can consider the role of technology in society and their responsibility as creators and consumers of media.

Comparing AI and human art cultivates an open and inquisitive mindset. Your students will become more discerning and sensitive to the human experiences reflected in all forms of creativity. They will start to see beyond the surface to deeper meanings and connections between the arts, ethics, and their place in an increasingly tech-infused world.

Art, regardless of its origins, is meant to be shared, interpreted, and used to understand ourselves and others better. That is the true power of bringing AI and human art together in the classroom for discussion and reflection. Students will develop a lasting appreciation for art as a profoundly human endeavor where artificial and natural intelligence contribute and evolve together.

BALANCING ALL THINGS

With exciting new possibilities comes responsible innovation. AI-generated art raises important questions about originality, authenticity, and an overreliance on technology that must be addressed and resolved. The solution is to integrate AI art with traditional techniques and use its challenges as opportunities for learning. Balance, ethics, and human creativity remain essential.

Foster dialogue around responsible progress and the use of technology for good. AI should enhance human capabilities, not compete with them. Considerations include:

- **Originality:** Can AI art be truly original, or is it recombining human influences and styles? Discuss the role of authentic imagination and life experiences in creating meaning and how this relates to meaningful artwork.
- **Authenticity:** AI opens the door to manipulated or *deepfake* media and art. Analyze how to build trust and address the ethical challenges of new technologies.
- **Overshadowing Traditional Art:** AI art may be novel and highly engaging, but it also threatens time-honored skills and creative processes. Find balance through projects combining AI and human art or reverse engineering machine learning models.

Remember, it's crucial to balance AI art with human creativity, integrate regular art instruction, and use these challenges as topics for meaningful class discussions. Possibilities include:

- Create new art forms that are only possible with AI while honoring design fundamentals and artistic heritage.
- Use AI to reimagine traditional styles so more people can access, participate, and benefit from them.
- Apply AI art skills toward positive goals such as raising awareness of social causes or promoting healing and growth.
- Have humans and AI collaborate on art, not work separately. Guide AI tools but give them a creative role, just as students work together and support each other.

FINDING THE BEST SITES

Here are a few of the many AI-generated art sites that are accessible and easy to use and that offer help with prompting. When choosing an AI-generated art site for your classroom, remember to consider the needs of your students and the types of art that you want them to create. Tools include:

- **DALL-E 3:** This is a powerful AI-generated art tool that creates realistic images from text descriptions by OpenAI. It is still in its beta stage, but it's free to use for educational purposes.
- **Canva:** Canva's text-to-image AI art generator is a free tool available to all Canva users. Users simply type a text description of the image they want to create. The tool then generates a realistic image that matches the description.
- **Midjourney:** This is a generative artificial intelligence program that lets you dream it, type it, and see it. You use it to create unique and original images from natural language descriptions (prompts). For example, you can generate a mechanical dove, a psychedelic rainbow bouquet, or a futuristic city. You can create images within the Discord app or their newly released website, which is currently one of the best AI art generators. Note that there is a monthly usage fee.
- **Microsoft Image Creator:** This is an AI-powered image generator integrated with Microsoft Copilot and Microsoft Edge. You create images from words using AI and then share them with others. You can also use it in Microsoft Edge to place images into any input area that supports image insertion, such as social media posts, blog posts, and more. It is powered by DALL-E 3's images as of the time of this writing.
- **OpenArt AI:** A free AI-generated art website, it allows teachers to create and customize AI-generated art with their students for educational purposes.
- **Ideogram:** This tool is new as of the time of this writing, and it writes text accurately within the AI art it creates at a much higher rate than other current models. This makes it useful to educators.
- **Adobe Firefly:** This creative, generative AI engine lets you dream it, type it, and see it. Teachers create unique and original content for their

lessons, presentations, and projects with simple text prompts. For example, you can recolor images, fill gaps, generate vectors, and more.

- **Stable Diffusion XL:** This Large Language Model was developed by Stability AI and generates realistic and creative images from text descriptions. It's based on the latent diffusion model, which is a type of deep generative artificial neural network.

STARTING SIMPLE, GROWING BIG

A few last tips ...

Start with simple prompts. When you are first experimenting with AI-generated art, it's helpful to start small. This will help you and your students get a feel for how the tool works.

Be creative! Bravely experiment with different prompts and see what kind of art you can create. The possibilities are endless!

Here are beginner prompts for teachers to use to create AI-generated art on these sites:

- A happy dog wearing a hat, in the style of a cartoon.
- A landscape of mountains and lakes, in the style of Bob Ross.
- A portrait of Albert Einstein, in the style of Andy Warhol.
- A dragon flying over a castle, in the style of a fantasy book cover.
- A still life of fruits and flowers, in the style of impressionism.
- A collage of famous landmarks, in the style of pop art.

REBOOT

Education is fundamentally about opening doors for our students—doors to new ideas, skills, experiences, and opportunities. With AI-generated art, we are unlocking a new realm of creativity, technological literacy, and innovative thinking. AI-generated art teaches students about different cultures, historical periods, and scientific concepts. It also helps students develop their creativity and problem-solving skills. (If you want to dive further into this topic, please visit micahminer.com and take the AI self-assessment rubric.)

So, friends, let's wield the brush of AI and provide our students with the freedom to explore a new artistic frontier created by their own vision and voice.

Let's not just teach art—let's pioneer the art of teaching in the age of AI. Remember, technology is a tool. It's not about replacing human creativity but enhancing it. And who knows? Maybe your classroom will produce the next *Portrait of Edmond de Belamy.*

Chapter 8
Moving into the AI Neighborhood

Our intelligence is what makes us human,
and AI is an extension of that quality.

— *Yann LeCun, computer scientist and AI researcher*

Image 8.1: Welcome to AI Metropolis!

With AI systems generating creative works, questions around copyright, bias, and responsible innovation are emerging and require answers. Discussions on AI's impact and relationship with human abilities shape how new technologies will develop. While AI amplifies creativity, our values like empathy, life experiences, and imagination remain uniquely human. AI becomes a tool for expressing human creativity rather than competing with it (see Chapters 3 and 7 for more).

As educators, it's crucial that we develop our own AI literacy so we can guide our students in this emerging landscape. Let's survey key AI principles, applications, ethics and responsibilities, and educational strategies to lay a foundation for AI-powered education. Then, we'll explore the applications based on how these tools work, dive deeper into ethics and responsibilities, and end with educational strategies to practice and apply in our classrooms.

It's time to consider your bold move into the world of AI. Imagine we're on a whirlwind tour of AI Metropolis, an exciting city filled with bustling neighborhoods, each representing different AI technologies that power innovations today. As you explore, you'll grow in your understanding of complex topics and learn real-world applications of how AI works. You'll also gain helpful tools to communicate about AI with your students and colleagues.

Can I Have a Quick Overview of the AI Inner City First?

As your friendly tour guide, I'll help you review the landscape, explore AI Metropolis, and take those first steps toward AI adoption.

Just like most modern cities are built on a solid foundation with meticulous planning, the world of AI has four basic strategies for its successful integration into your classroom (see Image 8.2):

- principles
- applications
- ethics and responsibility
- educational strategies

Image 8.2: Basic strategies for AI classroom integration.

We've glanced in the windows of these strategies in previous chapters, but here's a quick review before we begin our extensive tour.

STARTING OUR TOUR FROM THE AI PRINCIPLES MEETING PLACE

In the bustling heart of AI Metropolis lies the City Center, a place where the foundational principles of generative AI come to life. Here, algorithms and machine learning models interact like intricate systems of urban planning and governance, driving the city's (AI's) functionality and evolution.

Algorithms: The Architectural Blueprints of AI Metropolis
In our City Center, algorithms are like the city's architectural blueprints. They define the structure and flow of the city, determining how information travels and is processed. Just as architects design buildings, AI developers design algorithms to guide the AI's decision-making process.

Delving into the design of these algorithms is akin to exploring the detailed urban plans of a city. Each algorithm is crafted with a specific goal, whether it's to generate text, analyze data, or recognize images. These algorithms are structured to navigate the complex landscape of data and make informed decisions.

To illustrate, consider the Large Language Models (that operate like the city's information centers), analyzing and disseminating information (text) in a coherent and contextually relevant manner.

Machine Learning Models: The Brain of AI Metropolis

In our city analogy, neural networks represent the intricate system of roads and pathways, connecting various parts of the city and facilitating the flow of information. These networks, made up of nodes like brain neurons, process and transmit data ... it's the traffic moving through our city.

The training of these MLMs is similar to a city evolving through experiences. Just as a city learns to adapt to new challenges and changes, these models learn from both labeled and unlabeled data, gaining insights and skills over time.

Deep learning in AI can be compared to the multilayered infrastructure of a modern metropolis. These layers allow the city (AI model) to process more complex, nuanced information, such as deciphering intricate patterns in speech or images. Let's quickly explore the side alleys of three kinds of MLM learning:

1. Supervised Learning: The Structured District of AI Metropolis

In the Supervised Learning District, the city's development follows a well-planned, structured approach. Here, AI models learn from labeled data, similar to having clear guidelines and blueprints. This data comes with answers (labels), like a map that tells you the name of every street and building.

Compare the training process in this district to educating a student with a textbook that has both questions and answers. The model learns to make predictions or decisions based on this complete information and is evaluated by designers and other humans on how well it can apply this knowledge to new, unseen data.

2. Unsupervised Learning: The Exploratory Sector of AI Metropolis

The Unsupervised Learning Sector is the city's experimental zone. Here, AI models explore unlabeled data and learn to identify patterns and structures on their own. It's like exploring a city without a map, where the AI makes sense of its surroundings through observation and discovery.

This process involves AI grouping data into clusters, finding commonalities, or identifying unusual patterns, much like a city planner organizes a city into different zones based on their characteristics and uses.

3. Reinforcement Learning: The Dynamic Arena of AI Metropolis

In the Reinforcement Learning Arena, AI models learn through trial and error, guided by feedback from their actions. This is like learning to navigate a city by trying different paths and adjusting based on the success of each journey.

The model makes decisions and receives feedback in the form of rewards or penalties. Think of a city guide who learns the best routes and strategies over time by understanding which paths lead to rewards (efficient travel) and which lead to penalties (delays or problems).

Important stuff: The interaction between algorithms and machine learning models in AI Metropolis is like the interplay between city planning (algorithms) and the city's functioning (machine learning models). The plans guide the development and evolution of the city, while the city's functioning provides feedback to refine these plans.

Data District: The Building Blocks of AI's Knowledge

Data sets are the raw materials of AI. This section explores the variety and importance of data, emphasizing our need for diverse, comprehensive, and representative data sets. Chapter 3 covers how biases in data can lead to biased AI behavior, highlighting the importance of ethical data collection and curation.

Before AI learns from data, the information must be processed. This involves data cleaning (removing inaccuracies or duplications), normalization (standardizing formats), and categorization.

Ethical AI Principles: The Government District

Ethical principles are similar to the laws that maintain order and fairness within our AI Metropolis. While we discussed ethics in Chapter 3, this issue warrants another mention of the complex realities and alignment structures of the various generative AI models and companies. These guidelines, which vary by company, are not yet bound by universal laws to ensure that AI's growth aligns with the values of transparency, fairness, and inclusivity, shaping the technology to benefit society as a whole.

> After you have become more comfortable with AI tools, lend your voice to make wise decisions in your schools and other areas where you have influence.

The lack of guiding ethical AI principles is a political challenge at the local, state, national, and international levels. The advantage is that there's room for local decision-making and consensus-building within and across schools, districts, and state legislative agencies. After you have become more comfortable with AI tools, lend your voice to make wise decisions in your schools and other areas where you have influence. This builds AI literacy awareness and helps everyone collectively make better decisions.

Creative and Artistic District: The Manifestation of AI's Ingenuity

In the Art District, you showcase AI's ability to generate new, original content in text, image, video, code, and other outputs. The various forms of AI-generated content range from written works to visual art, lesson plans, tiered reading instruction, small-group learning, tutoring, writing assistance, and creativity boosts. Content generation and pedagogical supports that generative AI tools create with your prompting arise from this place, and the iterative process of AI learning is explored here. AI systems use feedback to refine and improve their outputs, drawing parallels with how humans learn from experience.

The Creative and Artistic District draws all areas together. AI Metropolis thrives on interdisciplinary collaboration, where different fields like healthcare, arts, and business intersect, creating vibrant and diverse neighborhoods. This integration showcases AI's versatility and its capability to enhance human endeavors across various domains.

USING APPLICATIONS TO GUIDE YOUR WAY

When you apply these principles to teach AI literacy, your educator creativity is set free to roam and explore. The first set of applications and project ideas for AI starts with teacher-centered generative AI applications to create text, images, music, coding, and the emerging field of generative video. This is where it helps to know the different AI tools (especially the free ones) and simply allow our educator brains to explore. Take instructional risks and try new ideas to engage your students with content and build their AI literacy skills.

Remember to be transparent when working with AI tools; students should know that you prompted an AI tool to help them learn a topic, skill, or vocabulary. In addition to using AI ethically, you're also teaching them how to properly, transparently, and ethically use the tools to help themselves and others.

Now, let's explore AI tools that help you create lessons, differentiate, translate, brainstorm small-group lessons, provide feedback on student writing, and so much more.

AI Teaching Assistants: Transforming Educational Practices and Teacher Efficiency

One application that can be helpful to teachers is an AI teaching assistant. AI assistants like **Class Companion**, **Magic School AI**, and **Eduaide** represent the emerging wave of technologies designed to bring generative AI tools with guardrails modified for the classroom. They offer promising avenues for reducing educator workload, personalizing student learning experiences, and enhancing overall educational efficiency. When embracing these AI tools, it's crucial to balance their integration with traditional educational methods, ensuring a harmonious blend of technology and human-driven pedagogy.

Following are a few examples of these tools at the time of this writing. There will be more, and the access and titles of the companies may change, but the point is the same: AI teaching assistants are excellent for providing student writing feedback and grading. These tools also help design lessons, offer assessments, tier instruction, simplify Lexile levels for reading instruction, provide small-group ideas, create rubrics, and help with many other tasks.

Although it's not exhaustive, here's a list of assistants. Experiment with them and see how they can help you with teaching and learning:

- **Class Companion:** Personalizing Feedback for Student Writing

  This AI teaching assistant specializes in providing personalized feedback on student writing assignments. It supports self-paced learning by allowing students to submit work, receive AI-generated comments, and revise their work accordingly. Class Companion also has demonstrated its utility in enhancing the learning experience across various subjects. Use rubrics for student learning from its library or upload your own. It multiplies teacher capabilities by providing timely, individualized feedback.

- **Magic School AI:** Streamlining Content Creation and Administrative Tasks

  Magic School AI is a versatile tool that assists in creating content, assignments, and documentation. Its unique features include a rubric generator, an Individualized Education Program creator, and a text-leveling tool, along with proofreading capabilities.

  By offering insights into student progress and reducing time spent on administrative tasks, Magic School AI significantly lightens the workload for educators. Its free accessibility makes it a valuable resource for schools.

- **Eduaide:** Helping Educators with AI-Enhanced Resources

  Created by public school teachers, Eduaide is tailored to address educator burnout. It provides an array of tools for planning lessons, creating teaching materials, and building assessments. It has free and paid versions, and the easy interface provides you with a quick way to brainstorm lesson and unit ideas, create rubrics and assessments, target certain student groups for instruction, support literacy efforts, and many other daily-grind elements of curriculum design and planning.

AI-Generated Music and Art: Creatively Engaging Students

We discussed AI art in-depth in Chapter 7, but many generative AI start-ups—in addition to well-known companies like Google and Microsoft—are exploring ways to create AI music. Although they vary in length and complexity, just think of how you can apply these tools in your classroom. How can you leverage this tool to engage your students and help them learn?

For instance, **Microsoft Copilot**, known primarily as an AI assistant, incorporates **Suno**, a tool designed for music composition. Suno's capability to transform text prompts into full musical compositions may revolutionize history as well as music education and other subjects.

Suno is a free tool you access through Microsoft Copilot. Simply create a prompt, such as, "I would like to have you write a song by using Suno about _____ in the style of _____ " and watch as something amazing emerges.

Here's an example: As a middle school social studies teacher, you might prompt Suno with, "Write a song about the Civil Rights Movement." This leads to the creation of a musical piece that reflects the struggles and aspirations of that era. You pair the results with topics from that time, including boycotts, sit-ins, and race riots, giving your students a deeper, more empathetic understanding of historical events.

Using AI to generate content like songs or artworks about specific historical events or eras serves as a powerful teaching tool. You bring abstract concepts to life, making them more relatable and understandable for students.

You can also use them for creative projects. Students could use Suno to create their own music and combine it with art based on the same theme, facilitating a deeper engagement with the subject matter and encouraging creative expression. Using AI to generate music and art is a win-win. Educators dramatically enhance their historical and cultural teaching, and students receive a unique understanding of different time periods and cultural contexts.

AI-Powered Video Generation: Current Landscape and Future Urban Sprawl

While AI-powered video generation is still evolving, its potential to transform educational experiences is undeniable. Educators who experiment with these tools can now lead the way in integrating innovative technologies into their teaching, paving the path for future educational advancements.

First, explore a few of the current leading platforms:

- **Google tools:** Google is also working on a series of video creation tools, but as of this writing, they have not been released to the public for testing yet. They are also creating a video game maker using AI called Genie, which will generate video game experiences based on user prompts.
- **OpenAI's Sora:** This is by far the best one out there at the time of this writing. It can create accurate videos up to a minute long with many

different styles, from realistic to anime, with movie-like quality. Soon it will be ready for the general public.

- **Pika Labs AI:** This offers an accessible platform for creating short, animated videos using text prompts. Its simplicity and range of styles make it an ideal tool for various educational purposes, despite variability in output quality.
- **Runway:** Known for its user-friendly interface, Runway provides a suite of AI creative tools, including video generation. Its full capabilities in educational settings are yet to be fully explored, but it shows promise.
- **Stable Video Diffusion by Stability AI:** This represents a significant leap in AI video generation, producing high-fidelity videos from single images. Its potential for creating detailed educational visuals is immense, although it's currently still under development and, at the time of this writing, is not accessible to the general public.

Second, envision future classroom applications:

Even though these emerging generative AI tools are new and still under development, educators can dream about the different ways they can use them to introduce, reinforce, or assess learning. Following are ideas that come to mind for application, but as you think about them in relation to the subjects you teach, your creativity and experience will find amazing ways to use these tools when they are ready for classroom use.

- **Integrate Emerging AI Video Generation in Your Future Classroom:** Soon, it'll be easy to create targeted definitions and provide images or visuals to help students learn. Or to create examples and non-examples using AI art's text features and generative images to reinforce academic vocabulary words for special education or English learners using a targeted Frayer model.

How about future scenarios?

- *History and Social Studies:* Create AI-generated videos to bring historical events or cultural narratives to life, enhancing your students' comprehension and engagement.
- *Science and Mathematics:* Use these tools to visualize abstract concepts, experiments, or mathematical theories in a more tangible form.
- *Language Arts and Foreign Languages:* Aid language learning and literature studies through animated adaptations of vocabulary words or language-based scenarios.

- *Creative Projects and Expressions:* Enable students to convert their ideas, stories, or project concepts into dynamic videos, fostering creativity and digital literacy.
- *Student Engagement and Creativity:* Revolutionize how your students interact with and understand complex subjects, offering new avenues for engagement and creative expression.
- *Digital Literacy and Skill Development:* Work with AI-powered video generation tools to enhance your students' digital literacy, preparing them for a technology-driven future.
- *Pedagogical Innovation:* Leverage these tools to create more dynamic and interactive learning experiences, making abstract or challenging topics more accessible and enjoyable.

So, How Can I Use All These Fresh and Innovative Materials in My Classroom?

NAVIGATING THE PRECARIOUS SUPERHIGHWAY OF ETHICS AND RESPONSIBILITIES

But what about authorship and ethics? With AI systems generating creative works, questions around copyright, bias, and responsible innovation emerge. Discussions on AI's impact and relationship with human abilities shape how new technologies develop. While we may amplify creativity, values like empathy, life experiences, and imagination remain uniquely human. AI is a tool for expressing human creativity, not competing with it.

As educators, we are responsible for teaching students so their young, impressionable minds learn the required skills to be successful humans. We try to guide them in finding their talents and interests. We also try to help them improve in the areas where they need more help, focus on topics that don't interest them but which they still need to learn, and practice skills that they struggle with.

The challenge with AI is that as it grows and evolves as a tool, students and educators can use it to complete tasks or activities they need to strengthen or are not interested in learning. It's done quickly, quietly, and craftily so no one else knows that a task was completed with AI. It's hard to detect or to define if it was plagiarism or cheating or simply counted as research. This is the area where many educators, for good reason, are wary of AI. This soundly falls in the lanes of the AI Ethics and Responsibility Superhighway.

In some cases, even as educators, we find ourselves tempted to take short-cuts and not do tasks ourselves but let AI do the boring work for us. This, too, is an important ethical dilemma, but there's also a difference between pla-giarizing (review the "6 Tenets of Postplagiarism" in Chapter 6) and realizing that since AI is a new tool, you may feel ashamed, skeptical, or as if you're cheating by employing it for repetitive tasks.

Here are a few suggestions to navigate this successfully:

- Be sure you're not in a blind spot.
- A good rule of thumb: When in doubt, be transparent about what and when you use these tools. That is, practicing good ethics and guidelines about how we as a society use these tools as methods to upskill quickly, democratize knowledge access, and increase the speed of task completion. A personal assistant helps us coordinate plans, and a virtual thought partner helps us think through an idea, an issue, or a lesson plan.
- Share the road.
- It's important not to have double standards. If AI tools make you a better teacher, why would you not want your class to use them to become better students? As a best practice, provide them with opportunities to practice using AI during your teaching, support conversations about it, and plan activities around AI literacy. In both cases, leverage AI tools to help with teaching and learning, and be transparent about when and how you use them in order to follow the ethical and responsible road.
- Use the guardrails.
- This is another reminder of how vital it is for schools and educators to select student-friendly generative AI tools. That means the tool has created guardrails to protect your students (and you!) from potential biases and harm. It must be aligned to create only school-appropriate and developmentally appropriate content and to protect student data, as required by state and national laws. From a teacher and school perspective, having AI policies and procedures in place that

everyone is aware of helps create a learning environment that respects ethics, transparency, and responsibility ... as long as all stakeholders (educators, students, parents, and leaders) know and understand how and when to use AI tools.

IMPORTANT RESOURCES

Teaching AI and AI ethics in K–12 classrooms necessitates effective resources that bridge the gap between the technical and ethical aspects of AI.

Here are a few great resources for you and your students:

- MIT Media Lab's AI + *Ethics Curriculum for Middle School*: This is an open-source treasure trove that imparts knowledge about AI through interactive lessons and activities.
- Another MIT-sponsored AI initiative is called the Day of AI. It's a free program that provides K–12 teachers and students with curriculum and activities to learn about artificial intelligence and how it affects their lives. The program was developed by MIT RAISE and can be run at any time and in any format by educators. The program also invites teachers and students to join a global celebration of AI education in May each year by sharing their projects and participating in events. Day of AI is supported by various sponsors and partners and has reached thousands of educators and students around the world.
- The International Society for Technology in Education: ISTE is an organization that prepares students for the careers of today and tomorrow by integrating AI into K–12 classrooms. It has a dedicated site called *AI Exploration for Educators* that is accessible to everyone (even if they are not ISTE members). You'll find various resources, programs, and courses to help teachers and students learn about AI and its capabilities, risks, and ethical questions. Its "Hands-On AI Projects for the Classroom: A Guide on Ethics and AI," for example, provides frameworks and standards.

CONSTRUCTING NEW EDUCATIONAL STRATEGIES

The most important steps are to start with the fundamentals, focus on interactive and hands-on learning, use relatable examples, discuss issues around responsible innovation, and relate AI to students' interests or future careers.

With a conceptual understanding and firsthand experience building or engaging with AI systems, your students become actively involved in shaping tomorrow.

Key principles to remember:

- AI can enhance and expand our creative horizons but not match the human spark of ingenuity.
- Machine learning powers many generative AI and GAN models producing art, text, images, and video.
- With new possibilities come responsibilities to guide progress so everyone benefits.

Here are suggestions for teaching basic machine learning (ML), generative AI, and other AI principles to your students:

- Explain machine learning as teaching computers to learn on their own by using data to make predictions or decisions without being explicitly programmed. ML powers many AI systems today, including those creating art and music. Focus on real-world examples students can relate to, like recommendation systems or image classification.
- Teach generative AI as a tool that uses algorithms and neural networks to generate new content such as images, video, text, and music. AI models are trained on huge data sets; then they create entirely new instances mimicking those examples. Show students examples of generative art, music, stories, or videos and discuss how they were created by AI systems trained on human works.
- Introduce students to neural networks, the algorithms that enable machine learning and power AI models. Explain neural networks as algorithms structured like the human brain and nervous system. They *learn* to perform tasks by analyzing huge amounts of data. While complex, focus on the basics of inputs, weighted connections, and outputs. Provide visualizations and examples to demystify the concepts.
- Discuss bias and ethics. As students explore machine learning and AI, talk about issues like unfairness, lack of transparency, job disruption, and privacy concerns. Have them consider how to address bias and build more ethical, trustworthy AI systems. Discuss AI's impact on society and the responsibilities of its creators.

- Teach through interactive platforms and hands-on projects. Have students train and build their own machine learning models or artworks using user-friendly platforms like **Google Teachable Machine, Runway ML, or Anthropic's Constitutional AI.** Step them through the process of gathering data, building and training a model, evaluating its performance, and then generating new instances.
- Focus on visualizations and simulations. Help students understand complex ML and AI concepts by providing interactive visualizations that demonstrate how neural networks operate or how models are built and trained. Use simulations to show systems generating new images, music, text, or other content. Break down the abstract into the visible and experiential.
- Relate AI to students' interests. For example, are your students into gaming or movies? Discuss how AI powers character animation and visual effects. Explain recommendation systems for streaming media or gaming platforms. Are they into social media? Talk about how AI facilitates image recognition and generation on apps like TikTok and Snapchat. Make connections between AI and their world.

TAKING A BYTE OUT OF CHATBOTS

Image 8.3: Big bytes—in the classroom of tomorrow, curiosity meets code.

The digital revolution sweeping across education has ushered in new, exciting tools that are changing how we teach and learn. Among these tools, chatbots such as **Byte** (developed by CodeBreakerEdu) are emerging as an innovative method for enhancing learning. Byte is an AI-powered educational tool that uses OpenAI's **ChatGPT 3.5 Turbo** to assist teachers and students in various subjects, including social studies, science, ELA, and math.

Byte is accessed through the CodeBreakerEdu website and is designed for classroom use without requiring users to sign in or collecting their data. That means it's safe to use in educational settings when you're teaching about AI or as a reference to demonstrate how AI tools are used to promote instruction. This respect for privacy aligns perfectly with our journey of navigating the brave new world of AI in education, where safeguarding student information is of utmost importance.

> Learning from these resources and integrating them into your curriculum empowers your students to navigate a future where AI plays an increasingly crucial role.

Exploring the potential of Byte or similar chatbots while maintaining student privacy in the classroom opens up a plethora of opportunities, depending on your educational goals. Here are a few ways students can interact with Byte or a similar generative AI tool:

- **The Tutor:** Have students ask Byte about topics they're studying. From coding to science, Byte stands ready as an on-demand tutor.
- **The Creative Partner:** Encourage your students to write stories, poems, or even jokes with Byte. Watch how Byte transforms into a creative ally.
- **The Challenge Master:** Let Byte pose puzzles, riddles, and brain teasers. In this role, Byte reinforces learning through engaging challenges.
- **The Feedback Provider:** Enable students to get constructive comments on their work, with Byte offering feedback tailored to each student.

Before integrating Byte or a similar chatbot into your curriculum toolbox to promote AI literacy, take a spin with it yourself. Explore its capabilities, understand its features, and uncover how Byte best aligns with your teaching objectives.

If you are committed to using chatbots, remember the potential criteria to evaluate which ones work best in your classroom (see Chapter 2 for more info). Here's a quick summary:

- **Effectiveness:** Does the chatbot accurately answer questions and provide reliable information?

- **Engagement:** Does it stimulate and sustain student engagement and interest?
- **Personalization:** Can the chatbot adapt its responses to individual students' needs?
- **Ethics and Privacy:** Does it adhere to data privacy norms and promote fairness and inclusivity?

IMPORTANT RESOURCES

Learning from these resources and integrating them into your curriculum empowers your students to navigate a future where AI plays an increasingly crucial role. It's not too dramatic to say that they reinforce our position as torchbearers, guiding our students on a balanced path between AI's immense potential and the ethical challenges it presents. Here are a handful of especially helpful resources:

- **AI4ALL Open Learning:** This is a free online resource that provides curriculum and teacher guides for introducing AI education to high school students of any subject. The curriculum covers various topics such as AI and drawing, facial recognition, deepfakes, environment, dance, and ethics. Bonus: It's aligned with several educational standards and is designed to be interdisciplinary and accessible for beginners. AI4ALL Open Learning aims to increase access to AI education and inspire students to pursue AI careers.
- **AI4K-12:** Another extensive catalog of AI-related resources, AI4K-12, is a valuable go-to compilation that includes a wide array of curriculum materials, books, and competitions for K-12 students. A great resource on AI for educators, this organization offers *The Artificial Intelligence (AI) for K-12 Initiative*, which is jointly sponsored by AAAI (Association for the Advancement of Artificial Intelligence) and CSTA (Computer Science Teachers Association). The initiative is developing:
  - national guidelines for AI education for K-12
  - an online, curated resource directory to facilitate AI instruction
  - a community of practitioners, researchers, resources, and tool developers focused on the K-12 audience
- **Common Sense Education:** A nonprofit organization that provides educators and families with resources and guidance on how to use technology and media effectively and responsibly. One of their

collections is *AI Literacy Lessons for Grades 6–12*; it consists of eight quick lessons that introduce students to artificial intelligence and its social and ethical impacts. The lessons cover topics such as AI chatbots, AI bias, AI algorithms, and facial recognition. The collection also includes additional resources such as articles, webinars, and toolkits to help educators and students explore and use AI in schools. Common Sense Education aims to help students think critically about AI and its role in shaping the world we live in.

- **Teaching AI for K–12:** This is a portal for learning and teaching about artificial intelligence, exploring how machines perform tasks that require human intelligence. The website offers three main sections: Learning About AI, Teaching About AI, and Developing AI Curricula. The first section introduces basic information about AI, such as how it works and what it means. The second section provides a collection of resources for educators who want to teach AI to students in grades K–12, such as lesson plans, online courses, and software. The third section, coming soon, will help curriculum developers design and implement AI curricula for different levels and contexts. The website aims to help students and teachers better understand the promise and implications of AI and foster the development of AI skills and literacy.

- **The International Society for Technology in Education:** ISTE offers an array of resources such as courses, books, and programs to help you and your students navigate the AI landscape. These include Educator Guides specifically designed for elementary, secondary, elective, and computer science classes. This site also curates a plethora of programs, courses, books, blogs, and podcasts in multiple languages that you could incorporate into your lessons at any time when the projects and topics make sense. ISTE's site also has research guides, providing in-depth insights on responsibly and effectively integrating AI into education.

EXPANDING YOUR KNOWLEDGE BEYOND THE CLASSROOM

Google and Microsoft offer free courses on generative AI to help people better understand AI and its applications. Generative AI, which is evolving as a term to describe the AI tools discussed here (and everywhere else!), includes

ChatGPT, Google Gemini, Microsoft Copilot, and other tools created by Large Language Models.

- **Google Cloud Skills Boost:** This site offers several no-cost AI training courses, including "Introduction to Generative AI," which explains what generative AI is, how it's used, and how it differs from traditional machine learning methods.
- **Generative AI Skills Initiative:** Microsoft, in partnership with LinkedIn, has launched free introductory courses on generative AI. This initiative is part of Microsoft's Skills for Jobs program and provides a professional certificate in generative AI upon completion. The courses are available through LinkedIn Learning and cover introductory concepts of AI and responsible AI frameworks. By taking advantage of these free courses, you enhance your understanding of AI and its applications and prepare yourself for the growing demand for AI talent in various industries.

There are many other ways to learn about AI. Doing an internet search or reaching out to me or the many other people in this space using a trusted social network like LinkedIn or X (Twitter) will yield good results. Remember, free resources are available, so be wary of anyone asking you to pay for something when there are high-quality, free options.

Ugh! How Do I Find My Way around AI Metropolis When I Have Even More Questions Now?

Good! You should have questions.

As we weave generative AI into the fabric of educational experiences, it's crucial to approach it with a *technoskeptical lens*, a framework urging us to consider the potential benefits and pitfalls of this technology. Drawing from Krutka and Heath's (2023) insightful examination of ChatGPT and Neil Postman's (1995) foundational principles on technological change, here's an outline of key questions for educators and policymakers to ensure the responsible integration of generative AI in our schools.

By critically examining these questions and fostering open dialogue, we navigate the ethical terrain of generative AI in education, ensuring it empowers creativity, strengthens critical thinking, and fosters responsible citizens in a technologically driven world. See Image 8.4.

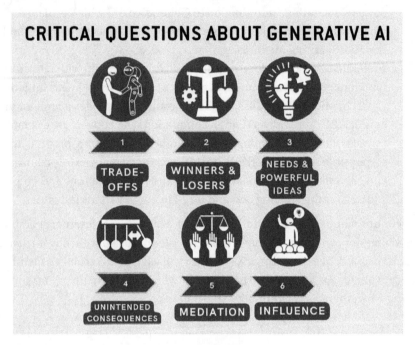

Image 8.4: Answer the questions before you begin.

1. CHARTING THE TRADE-OFFS

Generative AI promises to transform how students learn and how educators teach, offering unparalleled convenience and capabilities. However, every technological advancement involves trade-offs. What does society relinquish in exchange for these benefits? The ease of information generation and the automation of some tasks may inadvertently devalue the hard work and critical thinking foundation of meaningful learning. We must critically examine if this technology might create a culture of *shortcut learning* or undervalue the development of critical thinking skills.

2. BALANCING OUT THE WINNERS AND LOSERS

The widely adopted use of generative AI creates some winners and losers. In other words, it can further the power and wealth of the rich and already-privileged in a more profound way while separating others who are behind and marginalized, expanding the digital divide. It's crucial to identify who stands to gain the most from these advancements and who might be at a disadvantage, both now and in the long term, and then create policies and protections to mitigate this potential result. This extends to the classroom, where the digital divide might widen, affecting students' access to and engagement with these tools. Educators must work to ensure equitable access and bridge the digital gap to mitigate this risk.

3. PROTECTING CREATIVITY AND IDEAS

Generative AI introduces a paradigm shift in how ideas are created and owned. As its data-hungry algorithms fuel superpowered creativity, questions arise about the originality of creations and intellectual property ownership. This begs the question: How will this new technology that can create images, text, video, code, and so much more change our teaching and learning as well as society at large? Will it reshape our understanding of authorship and creativity, especially in disciplines that value original thought and analysis? We must explore the ethical implications of using AI-generated content and ensure safeguards are in place to protect originality and academic integrity.

4. UNCOVERING UNFORESEEN CONSEQUENCES

The broader societal implications of generative AI on jobs, privacy, and human interactions are profound. In education, especially in social studies and civics, what are the unintended consequences of relying heavily on AI? How does it impact students' understanding of history and democracy and their role as active citizens in a technologically advanced society? It's crucial to consider potential impacts on critical thinking, independent analysis, and responsible engagement with information.

5. MEDIATING LEARNING AND TEACHING

The mediation effect of generative AI on the educational process raises critical questions about its role in fostering or hindering critical thinking and creativity. How might generative AI impact the ways students learn and teachers teach, especially in subjects that demand a deep understanding of complex, nuanced historical and civic concepts? Educators must carefully consider how AI tools are used and ensure they promote, not hinder, the development of essential critical thinking and creativity skills.

6. UNDERSTANDING HISTORY AND DEMOCRACY IN THE AI AGE

Generative AI's influence extends to how students perceive knowledge, technology, and their understanding of historical and democratic processes. How does the use of AI shape their relationship with these concepts, potentially altering their engagement with and comprehension of history and democratic principles? We can foster critical thinking skills to evaluate AI-generated content and encourage our students to question, analyze, and engage actively with historical and democratic narratives.

REBOOT

To wrap up this chapter, let's touch on the three curriculum shifts you'll need for your big move to a more AI-infused world. The first curriculum shift includes the *potential bias* in generative AI based on the flawed data used to train it. Also included are the *ethics* of how, when, and where you use generative AI tools such as ChatGPT, Google Gemini, Microsoft Copilot, Claude, and others with submitted work (see Chapter 3 for a deep dive).

The second curriculum shift is *prompt engineering.* This is related to questioning, which is an important element in teaching and learning, and it focuses on helping you and your students ask the right questions for the best answers in generative AI (we discussed this in Chapter 4).

The third shift is about how we look at *assessment*. With AI tools getting smarter by the minute—they're even able to pass professional exams and tackle complex tasks now—it feels like we're standing at an exciting crossroads. That's why we have to start creating assessments that prioritize how students apply what they've learned to real-life situations (also covered in Chapter 6).

Our tour through AI Metropolis underscores generative AI's immense potential to transform teaching and learning. As your tour guide, I want to remind all educators that as this technology continues advancing rapidly, we have a profound opportunity and responsibility to integrate it with care and wisdom.

Understanding core AI principles, working with the applications, diving into curriculum resources, incorporating generative AI ethics and responsibility, and embracing technoskepticism to teach our students how to think critically help us separate hype from reality. Exploring creative applications inspires innovative educational uses, from AI teaching assistants to generative art and music projects. Examining ethical dilemmas grounds us in the discernment we need to prevent overreliance. Moving forward, transparency and balance will be key pillars of responsible AI integration.

We must be open about if and when we use AI tools, candidly discuss ethical trade-offs, and strike the right balance between harnessing benefits and preserving irreplaceable human elements in education. If you model generative AI literacy and use it thoughtfully, and if you provide your students the opportunity to interact with generative AI tools, then AI may free us from drudgery and expand creativity. However, we must always take care not to forfeit critical thinking and meaningful learning experiences for the expediency of automated education.

As AI shapes the landscape of learning, educators remain indispensable guides on this journey. By leading with vision, we create a future where AI elevates imagination, critical thinking, ethics, and empathy. Our students will then walk through this new technological terrain as empowered citizens, ready to harness AI for social good while retaining the agency to think independently. With care, wisdom, and discernment, we can fulfill generative AI's transformative potential to enrich education.

It's your move, intrepid traveler.

Chapter 9
Steering Confidently into the Future of an AI-Driven Classroom

What all of us have to do is to make sure we are using AI in a way that is for the benefit of humanity, not to the detriment of humanity.

— Tim Cook, CEO of Apple

Image 9.1: Digital companions—charting the path of AI in education.

As we step into an AI-empowered educational landscape, the transition represents a seismic shift rather than a gradual change. It demands new strategies and fresh ways of thinking from teachers. AI is here to stay, and the market for it—both in K–12 education and in other sectors of our personal lives, work, and society—will increase at exponential rates. That is why learning the basics and upskilling yourself now as educators can provide you with the tools to expand your skillset and apply it to your teaching and learning.

We can look into the future and know that AI will be expanding at an unprecedented pace. You can be at the forefront, confidently navigating this transformative journey with a well-honed AI skillset, or you can find yourself struggling to keep pace, using outdated educational practices in a classroom full of students ill-prepared for the future.

> Student instruction and enrichment should remain the ultimate focus of educators, and AI tools are only as good as how well we leverage them for student learning.

Remember our kindergarteners in our districts? Their entire K–12 educational experience will be in a world where AI tools are readily available, and their access, knowledge base, and intelligence will grow even more powerful. Thus, arming yourself with AI literacy and continuously enhancing your skills are more than just an investment in your professional development; they are equipping you to be a catalyst for transformative learning experiences that align with your students' present and future life experiences.

Yikes, This Is a Lot! How Do I Find My Way through the AI-Driven Maze?

Remember the LEAP framework we covered in Chapter 1 and expanded throughout the book? Here's a refresher:

- Learner-Centered
- Ethical Adoption
- Adaptive Personalization
- Performance Reflection

It's our guide to understanding these **new** tools and their impact on the educational landscape. It also serves as our compass as we explore three magnitudes of change in AI adoption: **status quo management, transactional change,** and **transformational change.**

STATUS QUO MANAGEMENT: AUGMENTING TRADITIONAL METHODS

Hey, change-makers! Picture this: You're at the threshold of the AI era in education. You're cautiously integrating AI into your existing toolkit, like sprinkling a dash of spice into a well-loved recipe. In your initial phases of using AI, cautious experimentation is key. Educators are slowly exploring the AI landscape, trying out new tools while maintaining current teaching results and pedagogical approaches. This is a soft launch—an incremental exploration rather than a wholesale overhaul.

- **Begin with the Basics:** The initial phase of embracing AI is marked by cautious curiosity, only scratching the surface of AI's potential. The primary objectives are to build foundational AI knowledge and foster confidence in this emerging tech. Understanding AI's core principles and cultivating faith in its prowess set the stage for a more profound AI immersion.

- **The Starting Line of AI Literacy:** AI literacy isn't just another trending hashtag; it's the cornerstone of integrating AI into your educational practices. Think of it as your compass in this new landscape, guiding you when, where, and how to utilize tools like ChatGPT or Google Gemini effectively. By understanding the mechanics behind AI, you empower yourself to use it as a magnifier for your teaching impact, not a substitute for your expertise.

> This isn't a phase; it's the new normal.

- **The Trust Factor:** Embarking on the AI journey is like starting a new relationship. You're filled with questions. Can I trust this generative AI tool? Will it help level up my teaching methods? Trust is built step-by-step. Once you learn how to leverage generative AI tools, they can cut down your administrative time, create content for lessons or differentiation, help you learn something new or how it can help others learn something new, and build more personalized learning for your students. Soon, you'll understand its role as a valuable team player for your educational goals.

Consider the suite of emerging generative AI tools we've examined in previous chapters, such as **ChatGPT, Google Gemini, Anthropic's Claude**, and **Microsoft Copilot**. These technologies hold promise to augment traditional lesson planning, grading, assessment design, and administrative paperwork that often overburden teachers. Used judiciously, they could reduce your non-instructional workload, freeing up time and energy for value-added mentoring. Do you want more education-specific tools? Try some of the many instructional AI tools we mentioned, such as **Brisk Teaching, SchoolAI**, and **Class Companion**, or research new and emerging AI tools created for education. Just remember to prioritize student data privacy, communicate with your administrators and IT departments, and make sure it is aligned with the LEAP framework or one you already use in your school or district.

No matter what, student instruction and enrichment should remain the ultimate focus of educators, and AI tools are only as good as how well we leverage them for student learning. This requires the proactive development of AI literacy among our teaching ranks. Let's cultivate a critical understanding of how AI systems function, how they appropriately enhance instructional practices without replacing the roles of human teachers, and how we transparently manage AI tools with care to prevent unintended harm, biases, or other consequences counter to our educational goals.

TRANSACTIONAL CHANGE: DIGGING DEEPER INTO AI INTEGRATION

You've passed AI 101 and are ready to take it to the next level. The goal now is to elevate your skills. It's like going from arithmetic to algebra; the foundational principles are the same, but the applications are more intricate and impactful. In the transactional change phase, AI shifts from an occasional support tool to a regularly integrated component of classroom instruction and school operations. Here, teachers employ thoroughly vetted AI tools much more frequently and creatively with the aim of measurably increasing educational efficiency, personalization, and learning outcomes.

- **Progressive Transition:** Now educators are not merely spectators but active participants, deepening their engagement. This phase epitomizes proactive and ethical immersion with AI. It's a period of evolution powered by data insights, where the spotlight is on harnessing AI ethically to enrich the teaching and learning trajectory.

- **The Ethical Compass:** Your accountability expands along with your use of AI. In addition to being a teacher, you are also a watchdog for responsible technology use. It is crucial—not optional—that these resources line up with the diversity, equity, and inclusion objectives of your classroom. At this point, you start considering how AI can be modified to be more than just a universally applicable solution.
- **We're All Students Here:** This phase marks a shift from AI as a tool to AI as a co-learner. As you gain insights into student performance and adapt your teaching strategies based on brainstorming, feedback, critical thinking, and a generative AI thought partner, you level up your teaching game. You're teaching your students while learning new ways to be more effective and insightful. This learning stage will always be here since AI breakthroughs are coming fast and aren't stopping. You'll always be learning something new both in AI and in teaching, so be happy you can be a student and keep learning.

Let's consider Google Gemini, for example. This new AI tool holds the potential to facilitate more diverse, equitable, and inclusive teaching and learning if implemented ethically. It translates classroom texts into dozens of languages, expanding accessibility for non-English-speaking students. Such capabilities align with the crucial principles of the LEAP framework (Learner-Centered, Ethical Adoption, and Adaptive Personalization) we've emphasized throughout the book, starting with Chapter 1.

Thoughtfully integrating AI necessitates continuous, careful evaluation. Educators must assess how well-adopted AI tools are for delivering on the promised effectiveness, accuracy, fairness, data privacy protection, and user-centered design in real-world school settings.

TRANSFORMATIONAL CHANGE: CHARTING NEW HORIZONS WITH AI

Hold on to your hats because this is where the educational landscape starts to look like a sci-fi novel—in the best way possible. At its most transformative, AI integration spurs a fundamental re-envisioning and redesign of education itself. Here, schools boldly employ AI capabilities to enable highly personalized, equitable, and innovative modes of learning. Rather than merely using AI as an efficient assistant, this level of integration requires interpreting and acting on the rich insights AI provides. Educators use these insights to re-evaluate and optimize teaching methods, organizational models, and educational objectives.

- **The Peak of AI Synergy:** At the pinnacle of AI assimilation, it seamlessly aligns as an educational ally, and classrooms morph into continuous learning ecosystems. This zenith redefines conventional teaching paradigms, placing AI at the heart of pedagogical processes. Here, the essence of AI in education comes to the forefront, unlocking its fullest potential.

- **AI as Your Co-Pilot:** Next, AI becomes your co-pilot, your teaching partner. It's not just about automating tasks; it's about seamless and student-centered AI integration for learning. Imagine real-time analytics that help you adapt lesson plans on the fly or AI-driven personalized learning paths that adapt to each student's unique learning pace and style. This is personalized education at its finest. This transformational approach aligns with the Performance Reflection principle we outlined in the LEAP framework (Chapter 1), pushing schools toward continuous improvement by harnessing new tools. It redefines teacher and student roles in an AI-powered classroom. Just as importantly, it positions educators as co-learners who constantly acquire new skills alongside their students through active professional development. Ultimately, AI integration facilitates human connections and equips learners for success.

- **The Infinite Learning Loop:** Both you and the game have changed. With AI, learning in the classroom is transformed into a never-ending journey of discovery and development. This isn't a phase; it's the new normal. You'll find yourself continually tweaking and refining your methods, fueled by the data and insights your AI co-pilot provides. You're now an AI pioneer, not just a user. You're asking questions that go beyond utility to transform the very fabric of education.

This is your moonshot moment. You're thinking big—beyond grades and test scores to life skills and holistic development. How can AI help your students become better problem-solvers, critical thinkers, and even human beings? As you navigate this transformative journey, remember: AI is the Jeep, you're the driver, and your vision is the roadmap. The most powerful tool in this journey isn't silicon; it's your mindset. Embrace AI as an ally in your pedagogical mission, and there's no limit to where you can go. You're not just adopting new technology; you're catalyzing a revolution in teaching and learning.

TAKING A LEAP: IT'S TIME!

In this journey of AI integration, remember that the LEAP framework serves as our compass, guiding us toward a future where technology and education merge seamlessly and foster an environment of enriched learning and growth.

Let's use LEAP to explore more deeply as we prepare for this brave new AI-impacted world:

- **Understanding AI (Learner-Centered):** Becoming AI-literate is the first step on our journey. Why? It's all about our students. As educators, our primary objective is to enhance their learning experiences. To achieve this in an AI-augmented environment, we must understand AI. We are defining AI as the capability of machines to mimic human intelligence, performing tasks like understanding natural language, recognizing patterns, and making predictions.

  As we have seen throughout *AI Goes to School*, AI tools like ChatGPT grade assignments, tailor lessons to individual students, and identify when a student is struggling with a particular concept, as discussed in Part 1. However, successfully integrating AI is not merely about implementing the technology but understanding how it enhances our teaching. Knowing AI's operations, terminologies, and ethical considerations equips us to identify how best to supplement our teaching methods and ensure that AI supports, rather than replaces, our human instruction for a learner-centered approach.

- **Evaluating AI Tools (Ethical Adoption):** Once we're equipped with a basic understanding of AI, the second step is to evaluate AI tools. This is an ethical step. AI tools, ranging from simple grading automations to sophisticated content and evaluation categorization and generation, are becoming increasingly prevalent in the classroom. As educators, our role is to ensure these tools are effective and ethical. Table 9.1 offers a rubric example to help you evaluate an AI tool (find a downloadable version at micahminer.com):

Criteria	1 (Weak)	2 (Fair)	3 (Good)	4 (Excellent)
Effectiveness	Results are inaccurate or irrelevant	Some inaccuracies present in results	Results are mostly accurate and relevant	Results are consistently accurate and relevant
Bias	Content contains insensitivity or prejudice	Some gaps in diverse representation	Most content is balanced and inclusive	Tool actively promotes diversity, equity, and inclusion
Data Privacy	No measures for data protection	Limited safeguards for data privacy	Robust data privacy protections are in place	Demonstrated commitment to data ethics with strong encryption, access controls, and transparency
Ease of Use	Interface is complex and poorly documented	Some parts of the interface are confusing or unclear	Interface is intuitive and well-documented	User experience is seamless with built-in guidance

Table 9.1: AI Tool Evaluation Rubric.

An ethical AI tool should promote diversity, equity, and inclusion; respect data privacy; and produce accurate, relevant results that enhance teaching and learning. For example, let's say a tool is effective at language translation, yet you must evaluate its adherence to data privacy norms and non-biased translations. Using a rubric to measure effectiveness, bias, data privacy, and ease of use ensures that your chosen AI tools align with your responsibility to provide a safe and inclusive learning environment.

- **Applying AI in the Classroom (Adaptive Personalization):** With a sound understanding of AI and a toolkit of ethically evaluated AI applications, you're now ready to bring these into your classroom. Picture a classroom where an AI tool, such as one that keeps student data private and safe and is a district-approved tool like Microsoft Copilot, offers personalized instruction tailored to each student's unique learning pace and style. And envision a setting where you automate administrative tasks, freeing up time for you to engage with your students more deeply. This is the potential of AI in education.

Aligning AI tools with learning objectives, generating educational materials, and streamlining administrative tasks transform education into an engaging, personalized experience, embodying Adaptive Personalization in the LEAP framework. This depends on knowing your students, finding ways to create learning experiences, and designing content to assist them in mastering what you're teaching by using more personalized instruction and reducing the barriers to engagement (see Chapter 6 and micahminer.com for more info).

AI tools allow you to maximize your planning and target what interests your students while still teaching them content. Here are several fun examples:

- Personalized readings from the topics and ideas students are interested in that also contain academic and content vocabulary.
- Rubrics for small-group work in reading or math.
- Lesson ideas or activities to differentiate for different reading levels, targeted tier groups, questions and sentence starters, and many other ways to support a more personalized student learning experience.
- AI-generated art that encourages interest and memory for academic and content vocabulary, specifically developed for EL students in the Frayer vocabulary model.

You already know what you need to do ... AI tools help you complete it efficiently.

- **Embracing the Evolving Role of Teachers (Performance Reflection):** Finally, we have a new role in an AI-enhanced educational landscape where we're not only providers of knowledge but also facilitators in a dynamic learning process. AI offers invaluable insights into student learning trends. This information, however, is only as valuable as our ability to interpret it and adapt our teaching methodologies accordingly. For example, using AI tools like ChatGPT, we can gather insights about our students' progress and adjust our teaching methods to enhance their learning experiences. This adaptation represents Performance Reflection in action. As education continues to evolve, we want our learning journey to be continuous, regularly updating our skills and knowledge to match the pace of change.

Important tip: Reflect on AI tools as you use them and as they evolve over time. What might have been a good use of AI tools for building up vocabulary words last week may not work for tomorrow's lesson on plot, character, and setting in reading. Exploring different perspectives on the Civil Rights Movement in a pretend press conference between Martin Luther King Jr. and Malcolm X last month may not be as relevant when you discuss the disparity between African American and white draft recruitments during the Vietnam War. The role-playing simulation you used to teach the hydrologic cycle in your previous science unit may not be useful for your photosynthesis project in this unit.

> Instead of being swept away by novelty, thoughtfully use AI tools to harness human-centered learning.

The good news about AI tools is that they are your virtual assistant, brainstorming partner, and educational collaborator as you reflect on what works and what doesn't, how to adjust your activity to differentiate or increase engagement, and how to prompt the AI tool for a better response. Happily, most AI tools create a history so you can reference what you used previously to help you refine and tweak it in the future. They are always ready to help, never get tired, and can be used to brainstorm any time, day or night. What an amazing impact they can have to improve teaching and learning!

NAVIGATING THE AI LANDSCAPE WITH A STUDENT-CENTERED PEDAGOGY

As innovative AI tools enter our classrooms, we must remain grounded in student-centered pedagogy. Before integrating any AI technology, pause and define your specific learning objectives. What skills or knowledge do you want students to develop? These pedagogical functions should guide your technology selection. Each part of your lesson from start to finish (whether or not they are AI-driven) should have a clear pedagogical function and a defined outcome or skill you want your students to acquire or practice.

For instance, if you seek to build your students' creative writing skills, choose tools that spark imaginative thinking, such as virtual mind-mapping, to brainstorm story ideas. Likewise, if your math students need more practice with word problems, identify AI apps providing interactive exercises at various levels. Adjust the difficulty as your students progress, keeping equity and inclusion at the forefront.

Rather than letting AI dictate classroom experiences, leverage it thoughtfully to meet defined pedagogical goals. Wield these powerful tools to awaken creativity, critical thinking, and the uniquely human strengths of your students. Approach AI with a clear vision, and continue letting student-focused teaching chart the course ahead. As we prepare for an AI-driven educational landscape, we must remain focused on our mission to facilitate learning. The introduction of AI offers us an unprecedented opportunity to redefine and reshape our classroom's educational experiences. While navigating this new landscape may be challenging, it's essential to remember—as we've learned from our own teaching experiences—that growth often comes from facing the greatest challenges.

What Key Strategies Will Help Educators Stay Adaptable and Informed?

In the ever-evolving landscape of K–12 education, generative artificial intelligence tools such as ChatGPT, Google Gemini, Microsoft Copilot, and Anthropic's Claude are transforming how we teach and learn. While these tools offer promising prospects for personalized learning, they also present unique challenges and ethical considerations that educators must address.

How can educators stay adaptable and informed? The answer lies in a blend of important strategies:

1. Build your AI literacy.
2. Purposefully integrate AI tools.
3. Empower students as digital citizens.
4. Influence community policies.
5. Commit to ongoing learning.

We've touched on all these points in previous chapters, and now here's a concise recap with clear steps, practices, and tips, with Image 9.2 as an easy reminder.

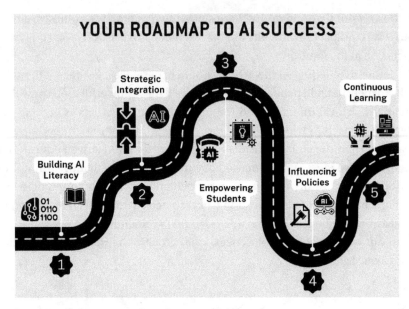

Image 9.2: Follow your roadmap for a smooth AI journey.

You can employ each of these strategies to stay up-to-date, effectively use these new AI tools, and leverage your voice on how, when, and where they are beneficial for students to learn and teachers to level up their instructional game.

STRATEGY 1 – BUILD YOUR AI LITERACY

As we voyage into the waters of AI, understanding the nature and capabilities of these tools is our first strategic move. Online resources, webinars, and communities offer valuable knowledge to unravel the mystery of how these AI tools generate human-like text.

However, our quest for AI literacy doesn't end here; it's an ongoing process. There is an element of capitalism and competition that we must consider since industry leaders and companies try to market to educators, public school districts, and other educational organizations. We must realize that AI tools will evolve with new startups or models replacing older established ones, such as the tools highlighted in this book. AI experts are continuously designing new models to surpass predecessors, so educators must regularly monitor new options through ongoing professional development.

How to Rock AI:
- **Action Steps:** Begin with the basics: read articles, join webinars, and participate in online communities focused on AI in education.
- **Continuous Learning:** Given the fast-paced evolution of AI tools, continuous professional development is vital. Consider participating in online courses or workshops to keep your knowledge up-to-date.
- **Big Tip:** The fundamentals of most generative AI tools and their applications are similar in principles. Pick an AI tool and play around with it yourself to feel comfortable and learn the basics. The tools will change and improve, but you'll have a solid foundation.

STRATEGY 2 – PURPOSEFULLY INTEGRATE AI TOOLS

The second strategy involves the cautious yet creative integration of AI tools into your classroom. Generative AI offers possibilities like automated essay writing and content creation, and these should be carefully aligned with your pedagogical goals. Instead of being swept away by novelty, thoughtfully use AI tools to harness human-centered learning. By strategically incorporating AI into your teaching and continually evaluating its effectiveness, you balance the exciting potential of AI with the time-tested best practices and pedagogies, instructional strategies, and impactful learning practices in education.

How to Rock AI:
- **Action Steps:** Pilot these tools, gather student feedback, and make data-informed decisions.
- **Continuous Learning:** Share what you've learned and listen to others about what they are doing.
- **Big Tip:** Update your assessments to include milestones and check-ins that are AI-proof, and be explicit on how and when your students can use these generative AI tools. (See Chapter 6 for more info.)

Educators across the country are focused on being transformative and trying to design new pedagogies and instructional practices to create more well-rounded and supportive teaching with AI. This is transformative terrain in education; take it step-by-step so you learn the basics, follow school policies, and don't get overwhelmed.

STRATEGY 3 – EMPOWER STUDENTS AS DIGITAL CITIZENS

Our next strategy revolves around the students. The AI journey isn't just for teachers; students need to understand the mechanics behind AI and be prepared to navigate its impacts. By offering hands-on projects and stimulating discussions, you expose your students to the principles that drive generative AI tools. This empowers them as informed, reflective AI users who can discern the implications of issues like misinformation and plagiarism. By encouraging students to ponder ethical considerations like biased algorithms and transparency, we're nurturing AI-fluent students and responsible digital citizens.

How to Rock AI:
- **Action Steps:** Teach students about data privacy, algorithmic bias, and the ethical use of AI tools.
- **Continuous Learning:** Incorporate hands-on AI projects that align with your curriculum.
- **Big Tip:** One of the hallmarks of being a good citizen is to be aware of the rules. What are your school and district's academic and acceptable use policies concerning AI? Learn them and then teach them to your students.

One great example is that my school district is incorporating AI principles into our Digital Citizenship curriculum as part of our Instructional Technology Coach roles and responsibilities. Our team co-planned lessons and ideas for the different grade levels based on ISTE's AI curriculum (found in Chapter 8) and other resources. In addition, we will participate every year in the Day of AI, just as we started observing the Hour of Code many years ago.

We are also piloting AI support for lesson plans by providing each teacher with access to a system that provides content- and grade-specific AI support. All educators and administrators will have access to this platform, and it will be supported by our instructional technology team members at each school. All of this is to provide access, guidance, and support to educators and students as we learn how these AI tools will impact our society. We are doing our best to prepare ourselves and our students for that change.

STRATEGY 4 – INFLUENCE COMMUNITY POLICIES

We can't navigate the adventures of generative AI without considering the larger picture of policies and regulations. Educators have a pivotal role in steering discussions about student protection, privacy, and equitable AI access. By actively participating in policy-making communities, we help shape guidelines that serve the best interests of students and educators, not just corporations. Protecting our profession from invasive data collection and monitoring, for instance, is an important part of the policy-shaping process.

How to Rock AI:
- **Action Steps:** Engage with policy-making bodies and educational boards to ensure that AI integration aligns with the best interests of your students and fellow teachers.
- **Continuous Learning:** Find a group of committed educators in your school or district, listen to podcasts or social media, and use your professional learning networks to reflect, learn, explore, and bounce ideas off in order to stay informed about AI challenges and innovative practices.
- **Big Tip:** Include sample letters or scripts that educators can use to communicate their concerns or suggestions to decision-makers (see micahminer.com for ideas).

My school district is updating our academic code of conduct and providing academic integrity policy recommendations for all its schools and class-rooms. Also, we will start the upper elementary and middle school grades using the CodeBreakerEdu safe chat link so students can experience AI, dis-cuss where and how the tools can be used, and learn how AI will be useful now and in the future. All school districts and educational organizations are in the process of making pedagogical and policy shifts in light of this new technology, so let's work together and network with others to make sure we can support our students in this seismic shift in education.

STRATEGY 5 – COMMIT TO ONGOING LEARNING

Finally, as we explore this new territory, open-ended learning will help us navigate. In the rapidly evolving world of generative AI, maintaining our adaptability and staying informed require a commitment to lifelong learning. Regularly engaging with professional development opportunities, research publications, and learning communities helps educators keep abreast of new developments and ethically harness innovations for the benefit of our students.

How to Rock AI:
- **Action Steps:** Set up your next professional development or personal development to focus on AI in education.
- **Continuous Learning:** Sign up for a newsletter, follow a social media site, or subscribe to a podcast to stay informed without having to do all the research yourself. Better yet, do all three.
- **Big Tip:** Find an organization, group, or team (maybe in your own school) where you can connect and share helpful tips and valuable info.

You have in your hands and at your fingertips a wealth of information on the ever-changing world of AI. This book provides plenty of resources on how to research, access, and use generative AI tools in the classroom and as part of your digital citizenship lessons. My website (micahminer.com) also offers many more free resources, continually updated articles, and ideas. In addition, you can sign up for my monthly newsletter; it keeps educators and educational leaders up-to-date with the newest educational AI changes. You're welcome to reach out to me anytime.

Many educators are already using these tools in effective and innovative ways. Use your professional networks and reach out to others. Access ISTE and other tools (highlighted in Chapter 8) that are free. They can help you keep up with the latest AI tools and resources. Remember: AI tools are not going away, and educators are lifelong learners, so take up this challenge as part of your professional responsibilities. You've got this!

REBOOT

Embarking on the AI journey in education is akin to setting out on a grand expedition across a vast and uncharted territory. We just finished a long journey through this book to help you get familiar with the new terrain. As we trek into an AI-infused academic landscape, educators must become the trailblazers, mapping the route toward a student-centered pedagogy. The compass that guides us through this terrain is our dedication to leveraging AI as a tool to amplify human potential rather than using it as a substitute for the personal touch of a dedicated teacher.

Your path is charted through a progression of key strategies—building AI literacy, creating strategic integration, empowering students, influencing policies, and committing to continuous learning. This route promises to transform your teaching methods and the very landscape of education itself.

In the same spirit of adventure and discovery, it's crucial to keep your gaze forward, embracing AI as a trusted companion in your educational odyssey. Your willingness to learn and adapt ensures that AI remains a valuable ally. And just as the journey is essential, so is the map—it represents a strategic guide that underscores every step of your passage through the intertwined worlds of AI and education.

As you stand on the brink of this AI-driven horizon, let this be your final word of advice for today: Embrace this future, make AI a powerful ally, and step forward with the confidence that you are leading the way. By integrating AI into your pedagogy, you are not only keeping pace with change but driving it, ensuring that your students are ready for the future and ready to lead it.

Conclusion
Okay, What's Next?

Technology's primary effect is to amplify human
forces, so in education, technologies amplify
whatever pedagogical capacity is already there.

— *Kentaro Toyama, computer scientist, professor,*
and development researcher

Image 10.1: Step out and find your way with generative AI tools.

As we conclude our shared exploration of the promise and potential of AI in education, let's revisit where our journey began. In the introduction, we foresaw the kindergarten students of today becoming the graduating class of 2035, entering a world profoundly influenced by artificial intelligence. The crucial question for educators is how we equip students for an AI-driven workplace and an AI-shaped society and life.

How can we empower them to be ethical, informed, and active architects of the technology they will inherit?

The resounding theme echoed throughout this book is balance. It's essential to counterbalance our enthusiasm for AI's possibilities with judicious skepticism about its risks and limitations. We need to strike a balance between effective automation and enduring human values, critical thinking skills and human relationships. And we must guide students to balance technological fluency with critical thinking, creativity, and wisdom that no AI tool can replicate. If AI tools really can be used to harness a human-centered education, they must augment our instruction to improve our human education and enhance our connections to humanity.

At its heart, education must be governed by human-centered pedagogy, not technology. While tools like ChatGPT, Google Gemini, Microsoft Copilot, and Claude might come and go, our fundamental goals as educators—to nurture, empower, expand minds, and touch hearts—remain the same. It's why the LEAP framework focuses on adopting AI tools that are learner-centered, have ethical applications, provide ways for us to personalize teaching, and depend on performance reflection.

We could add an "S" to the acronym to make it LEAPS, since student-centered pedagogy should drive what we do as educators. Thoughtfully using AI tools with students in mind to plan lessons, acquire feedback, and generate content must be driven by the relationships we build with our students to help them learn. New pedagogies will develop, along with research on best practices, but current best educational practices based on past educational theories and pedagogies still have a place, are relevant, and can be incorporated into this new AI-influenced educational landscape.

As I stated in the introduction and have echoed throughout *AI Goes to School*, the world of generative AI tools is changing in many ways, where anything you view, upload, or create will be accessible to AI tools. We've also briefly explained what instructional AI is and how tools like **Packback**, **Grammarly**, and **Khanmigo** use technology to provide personalized learning support. When you thoughtfully implement these platforms, they offer real-time writing feedback, interactive math guidance, and more ... helping you meet each student's unique needs.

Instructional AI aims to act as an adaptive tutor, not just a cold and dispassionate algorithm. The goal is to understand and nurture each learner through tailored guidance. Generative AI, on the other hand, creates novel content for educators in surprising and innovative ways, changing how students learn and you teach. With either type of educational AI tool, it's vital that you use it ethically and protect your students' privacy.

Looking ahead, there's a whirlwind of change in educational AI tools. There will always be something new, such as more finely tuned AI applications, as well as other tools that, at the time of this writing, have not been made public or are still a twinkle in an IT designer's eye.

That's to be expected and provides a great reason for us to continue researching, innovating, and learning. These powerful, new emerging systems allow users to generate content across modalities (text, images, video, audio, code, and so much more). Students create 3D interactive models to demonstrate concepts, while teachers automate administrative tasks, opening even more possibilities to engage students and support educators. Most exciting are the multimodal AI models that hint at a future where learners have creative autonomy at their fingertips. I predict that they will continue to be an arena for innovation across all industries, especially education.

However, integrating these rapidly advancing technologies into the classroom requires careful consideration of ethical implications and real educational value. How can multimodal AI enrich learning without over-automating or dehumanizing education? We must continue to have thoughtful and critical conversations from here on out, yet the principles of how AI works and how we—students, educators, and all users—interact with these tools will remain consistent and improve over time.

The scenarios, strategies, and reflections presented in this book are intended to provide a roadmap for leveraging AI as a tool for human progress, not as an impersonal force that shapes education with its own limitations. In practical terms, a human-centered vision of AI integration involves enhancing the elements that are fundamental to learning, such as creativity, critical thinking, empathy, and relationships. It's about creating opportunities for meaningful mentorship, deep engagement, and projects that engage the heart, hand, and mind. These are timeless and at the core of education, existing long before algorithms and enduring long after.

AI Goes to School is much more about nurturing natural human intelligence than it is about understanding artificial intelligence. If AI is to be a transformative force in education, we must first transform our vision of why we educate: to uplift humanity, build communities, and guide students toward lives of purpose.

Whether you're a tech enthusiast or skeptic, I hope you feel more empowered to navigate this technology wisely, continue to use critical thinking in anything new (especially with AI and technology), and lead with wisdom and your experience as an educator and human being. Always center your values on equity, ethics, and human dignity.

Start with small steps because trying something is better than doing nothing.

Remember, this change is a journey, not a destination. Keep your focus on the young lives under your care who look to you to guide them into an AI-driven future and to prepare them for their human futures as critical thinkers and positive and thoughtful members of our society. Education is an act of faith in our students' potential, creativity, and resilience. They will need this faith to navigate a future we can't fully envision yet. If our students view technology as a canvas that they can collectively shape, they will undoubtedly paint something beautiful.

AI Goes to School is just one guide; many other people are creating excellent resources and doing amazing work locally, nationally, and internationally. Use your networks to find them, learn, and share. Use what you learned here to integrate AI into your classroom, and then share your insights and experience with your peers. The challenges and opportunities of AI in education are best navigated together.

Empower your students to build the future they want to inhabit. This is not just about learning to use AI tools; it's about fostering a generation capable of using AI to serve the public good.

What you've read and learned here equips you with knowledge and strategies ... now it's time to act. Let's foster creativity and empower critical thinking to ensure that AI serves everyone, especially in our schools. Our students' future—and humanity's—depends on our collective actions today.

Let's choose wisely. Let's choose with our students in mind. They deserve nothing less.

Where Can I Find More?

I have so much to share with you that it won't fit in one book. The following resources are *free* and available to you at micahminer.com. Stop by often for updates, too!

Chapter Graphics
These graphics, discussed in detail in *AI Goes to School* chapters, are great visuals to remind you about steps, processes, and more. Feel free to download and use them.

Fun Images
Yep, you can also find (and use) some really fun images I've created for *AI Goes to School*, as well as for my presentations and keynote speeches. I have the rights to the images, and I'm sharing them with you. You're welcome.

Rubrics
Why reinvent the rubric when you can have one that's already made and waiting for you to use? Actually, there are several. Take a look and see what fits for you.

Resources
And, of course, I've got tons of sources to back me—and you—up. Stop by every once in a while, as I'll continue updating this list with more info on the latest regulations, trends, and Really Cool Stuff.

Templates
While you'll want to revise these for your district, school, and classroom needs, they're quick checklists that cover all the important stuff and start you on your happy way to AI integration.

Works Cited

While some people might think this section is only worth reading on a night they are battling insomnia, others may find the sources useful and noteworthy. No judging on my part; just sharing the info.

Also, I have *lots* more resources I'd like to share with you. Feel free to explore my website, micahminer.com. I'm always adding new sources, creating fun visuals, and posting the latest AI updates.

AI Use
I used DALL-E 3 to generate AI outputs from October 2023 to March 2024. It can be commercially distributed based on their Terms of Use at openai.com/policies/terms-of-use. Also, the guest forewords were written using OpenAI GPT-4, Google Gemini Advanced, Microsoft Copilot, and Anthropic Claude 3. All other text was written by me, Micah Miner.

References

Chapter 1

Anyoha, R. 2017. "The History of Artificial Intelligence - Science in the News." Sitn, August 28, 2017. https://sitn.hms.harvard.edu/flash/2017/history-artificial-intelligence/.

Doroudi, S. 2022. "The Intertwined Histories of Artificial Intelligence and Education." *Int J Artif Intell Educ.* https://doi.org/10.1007/s40593-022-00313-2.

Holmes, W., Bialik, M., and Fidel, C. 2019. Artificial Intelligence in Education: Promises and Implications for Teaching and Learning. The Center for Curriculum Redesign. https://curriculumredesign.org/wp-content/uploads/AIED-Book-Excerpt-CCR.pdf.

McKinsey & Company. 2022. "What are Industry 4.0, the Fourth Industrial Revolution, and 4IR?" https://www.mckinsey.com/featured-insights/mckinsey-explainers/what-are-industry-4-0-the-fourth-industrial-revolution-and-4ir.

Naudé, W. 2021. "Artificial Intelligence: Neither Utopian nor Apocalyptic Impacts Soon." *Economics of Innovation and New Technology* 30(1): 1–23. https://doi.org/10.1080/10438599.2020.1839173.

Chapter 2

AVID. 2023. "How Teachers Can Use ChatGPT - Discover Eight Ways That ChatGPT Can Benefit Teachers and Save You Time." AVID Open Access, February 9, 2023. https://avidopenaccess.org/resource/how-teachers-can-use-chatgpt/.

AVID. 2023. "Khanmigo as an AI Personal Tutor and Assistant." AVID Open Access, July 23, 2023. https://avidopenaccess.org/resource/khanmigo-as-an-ai-personal-tutor-and-assistant/#1684442733241-0aad33d6-5846.

ISTE. n.d. "Artificial Intelligence in Education." Accessed June 29, 2023. https://www.iste.org/learn/artificial-intelligence-education.

Open AI. 2023. "Models - OpenAI API. Platform." https://platform.openai.com/docs/models/overview.

OpenAI. 2023. "GPT-4 Technical Report." https://arxiv.org/abs/2303.08774v3.

Chapter 3

Akgun, S., and Greenhow, C. 2022. "Artificial Intelligence in Education: Addressing Ethical Challenges in K–12 Settings." AI Ethics 2: 431–440. https://doi.org/10.1007/s43681-021-00096-7.

Dieterle, E., Dede, C., and Walker, M. 2022. "The Cyclical Ethical Effects of Using Artificial Intelligence in Education." *AI & Soc.* https://doi.org/10.1007/s00146-022-01497-w.

ITEC. "Bridging the Gap between the Theory of Ethical Principles and the Practice of Technology Ethics in Organizations: The ITEC Primer." Markkula Center website, 2023. https://www.scu.edu/institute-for-technology-ethics-and-culture/itec-primer/.

Stone, Adam, and EdTech Magazine. "Student Data Privacy Laws: Understanding FERPA and CIPA." April 28, 2022. https://edtechmagazine.com/K–12/article/2022/04/understanding-ferpa-cipa-and-other-K–12-student-data-privacy-laws-perfcon.

U.S. Department of Education, Office of Educational Technology, Artificial Intelligence and Future of Teaching and Learning: Insights and Recommendations. 2023. https://tech.ed.gov/ai-future-of-teaching-and-learning/.

Chapter 4

Brown, T. B., et al. 2020. "Language Models are Few-Shot Learners." OpenAI. https://arxiv.org/abs/2005.14165.

Celik, I., Dindar, M., Muukkonen, H., et al. 2022. "The Promises and Challenges of Artificial Intelligence for Teachers: A Systematic Review of Research." TechTrends 66: 616–630. https://doi.org/10.1007/s11528-022-00715-y.

CoSN. 2023. "Artificial Intelligence (AI) in K–12 (Version 1.1)." Consortium for School Networking. https://www.cosn.org/wp-content/uploads/2023/03/CoSN-AI-Report-2023-1.pdf.

CoSN. 2023. "ChatGPT Above the Noise Member Brief." March 15, 2023. https://www.cosn.org/wp-content/uploads/2023/03/ChatGPT-Above-the-Noise-Member-Brief.pdf.

Chapter 5

AI Accelerator Institute. "5 Real-Life Use Cases of Artificial Intelligence in Education." Accessed September 4, 2023. https://www.aiacceleratorinstitute.com/5-real-life-use-cases-of-artificial-intelligence-in-education/.

Chen, C. 2023. "AI Will Transform Teaching and Learning. Let's Get It Right." Hai, March 9, 2023. https://hai.stanford.edu/news/ai-will-transform-teaching-and-learning-lets-get-it-right.

Garibay, O. O., et al. 2023. "Six Human-Centered Artificial Intelligence Grand Challenges." *International Journal of Human–Computer Interaction 39*(3): 391–437. https://doi.org/10.1080/10447318.2022.2153320.

IBM Research. "What is Generative AI?" Accessed September 4, 2023. https://research.ibm.com/blog/what-is-generative-AI.

Marr, Bernard. "How Is AI Used in Education - Real World Examples of Today and a Peek into the Future." Accessed September 4, 2023. https://bernardmarr.com /how-is-ai-used-in-education-real-world-examples-of-today-and-a-peek-into -the-future/.

Rouse, Margaret. "Generative AI (Generative Adversarial Network)." TechTarget. Accessed September 4, 2023. https://www.techtarget.com/searchenterpriseai /definition/generative-AI.

Shneiderman, B. 2023. "Human-Centered AI." *Issues in Science and Technology 39*(3): 62–65. https://issues.org/human-centered-ai/.

Steinbauer, G., Kandlhofer, M., Chklovski, T., et al. 2021. "A Differentiated Discussion About AI Education K–12." Künstl Intell 35: 131–137. https://doi.org/10.1007 /s13218-021-00724-8.

U.S. Department of Education, Office of Educational Technology. "Artificial Intelligence in Education: Promises and Implications for Teaching and Learning." Accessed September 4, 2023. https://www2.ed.gov/documents/ai-report /ai-report.pdf.

Chapter 6

Anson, C. M., and Straume, I. 2022. Amazement and Trepidation: Implications of AI-Based Natural Language Production for the Teaching of Writing. *Journal of Academic Writing, 12*(1), 1–9. https://doi.org/10.18552/joaw.v12i1.820.

Berson, I., Berson, M. 2023. "The Democratization of AI and Its Transformative Potential in Social Studies Education." *Social Education 2*(87): 114–118. https://www.socialstudies.org/social-education/87/2/democratization-ai -and-its-transformative-potential-social-studies-education.

Chang, C.-H., and Kidman, G. 2023. "The Rise of Generative Artificial Intelligence (AI) Language Models - Challenges and Opportunities for Geographical and Environmental Education." International Research in Geographical and Environmental Education. https://doi.org/10.1080/10382046.2023.2194036.

Eaton, Sarah Elaine. "6 Tenets of Postplagiarism: Writing in the Age of Artificial Intelligence." Dr. Sarah Elaine Eaton's Blog. February 25, 2023. https://drsaraheaton.wordpress.com/2023/02/25/6-tenets-of-postplagiarism -writing-in-the-age-of-artificial-intelligence/.

Krutka, D. G., Metzger, S. A., and Seitz, R. Z. 2022. "'Technology Inevitably Involves Trade-Offs': The Framing of Technology in Social Studies Standards." *Theory and Research in Social Education, 50*(2): 226–254. https://pure.psu.edu/en /publications/technology-inevitably-involves-trade-offs-the-framing-of-technolo.

Krutka, Daniel G., Heath, Marie K., and Mason, Lance E. 2020. "Technology Won't Save Us: A Call for Technoskepticism in Social Studies." *Contemporary Issues in Technology and Teacher Education, 20*(1). https://citejournal.org/volume-20/issue-1-20/social-studies/editorial-technology-wont-save-us-a-call-for-technoskepticism-in-social-studies.

Miller, M. and Ditch That Textbook. "ChatGPT, Chatbots and Artificial Intelligence in Education." December 17, 2022. https://ditchthattextbook.com/ai/#tve-jump-18606008967.

Wieck, Lindsey Passenger. "Revising Historical Writing Using Generative AI: An Editorial Experiment." Perspectives on History, August 15, 2023. https://www.historians.org/research-and-publications/perspectives-on-history/summer-2023/revising-historical-writing-using-generative-ai-an-editorial-experiment.

World Economic Forum. "ChatGPT and Cheating: 5 Ways to Change How Students Are Graded." March 31, 2023. https://www.weforum.org/agenda/2023/03/chatgpt-and-cheating-5-ways-to-change-how-students-are-graded/.

Chapter 7

Fang, X., Ng, D. T. K., Leung, J. K. L., et al. 2023. "A Systematic Review of Artificial Intelligence Technologies Used for Story Writing." *Educ Inf Technol.* https://doi.org/10.1007/s10639-023-11741-5.

Garcia, Chris. "Harold Cohen and AARON: A 40-Year Collaboration." Computer History Museum, April 27, 2016. https://computerhistory.org/blog/harold-cohen-and-aaron-a-40-year-collaboration/.

Vartiainen, H., and Tedre, M. 2023. "Using Artificial Intelligence in Craft Education: Crafting with Text-to-Image Generative Models." Digital Creativity. https://doi.org/10.1080/14626268.2023.217455.

Zhang, H., Lee, I., Ali, S., DiPaola, D., Cheng, Y., and Breazeal, C. 2022. "Integrating Ethics and Career Futures with Technical Learning to Promote AI Literacy for Middle School Students: An Exploratory Study." International Journal of Artificial Intelligence in Education. https://doi.org/10.1007/s40593-022-00293-3.

Chapter 8

Chen, C. 2023. "AI Will Transform Teaching and Learning. Let's Get it Right." Hai. https://hai.stanford.edu/news/ai-will-transform-teaching-and-learning-lets-get-it-right.

CoSN. 2023. *Artificial Intelligence (AI) in K–12.* Consortium for School Networking. Spring 2023, Version 1.1. https://www.cosn.org/wp-content/uploads/2023/03/CoSN-AI-Report-2023-1.pdf.

ISTE. "Artificial Intelligence in Education." Accessed September 3, 2023. https://beta.iste.org/artificial-intelligence-in-education.

Krutka, Daniel G., and Heath, Marie K. 2023. "Asking Technoskeptical Questions about ChatGPT." Civics of Technology. April 2, 2023. https://www.civicsoftechnology.org/blog/asking-technoskeptical-questions-about-chatgtp.

Kukulska-Hulme, Agnes, et al. 2023. "Innovating Pedagogy 2023: Open University Innovation Report 11." The Open University. Innovating Pedagogy | Open University Innovation Reports.

Kumar, M. J. 2023. "ChatGPT is Not What You Think It Is." *IETE Technical Review,* *40*:1, 1–2. https://doi.org/10.1080/02564602.2023.2187976.

Mollick, Ethan. "What Can be Done in 59 Seconds: An Opportunity (and a Crisis): Five analytical tasks in under a minute." One Useful Thing, January 31, 2024. https://www.oneusefulthing.org/p/what-can-be-done-in-59-seconds-an.

OpenAI. "Teaching with AI." OpenAI Blog. August 31, 2023. https://openai.com/blog/teaching-with-ai/.

Preetham, F. 2023. "Mathematically Evaluating Hallucinations in LLMs Like GPT4." Medium, March 18, 2023. https://medium.com/autonomous-agents/mathematically-evaluating-hallucinations-in-llms-like-chatgpt-e9db339b39c2.

Sanusi, I. T., Oyelere, S. S., Vartiainen, H., Tedre, M., and Asino, T. I. 2022. "A Systematic Review of Teaching and Learning Machine Learning in K–12 Education." Education and Information Technologies. https://doi.org/10.1007/s10639-022-11416-7.

Selwyn, Neil. 2024. "On the Limits of Artificial Intelligence (AI) in Education." Nordisk tidsskrift for pedagogikk og kritikk 10: 3–14. https://doi.org/10.23865/ntpk.v10.6062.

Chapter 9

Drost, Bryan R. "Pedagogy Before Technology." Educational Leadership. December 2021/January 2022. http://www.ascd.org/el/articles/pedagogy-before-technology.

Frontier, Tony. "AI and Education: The Importance of Asking Big Questions." *Educational Leadership* 79:4 (December 2021/January 2022): 42–47.

Krueger, N. 2023. "What Educators and Students Can Learn From ChatGPT - ISTE Blog." ISTE, February 23, 2023. https://www.iste.org/explore/artificial-intelligence/what-educators-and-students-can-learn-chatgpt.

U.S. Department of Education, Office of Educational Technology. 2024. *A Call to Action for Closing the Digital Access, Design, and Use Divides.* 2024 National Educational Technology Plan. https://tech.ed.gov/files/2024/01/NETP24.pdf.

U.S. Department of Education, Office of Educational Technology. 2023. *Artificial Intelligence and Future of Teaching and Learning: Insights and Recommendations.* https://tech.ed.gov/ai-future-of-teaching-and-learning/.

Vartiainen, H., and Tedre, M. 2023. "Using Artificial Intelligence in Craft Education: Crafting with Text-to-Image Generative Models." Digital Creativity. https://doi.org/10.1080/14626268.2023.217455.

About the Author

M icah Miner, MA, MEd, EdS, has presented keynote speeches and served as a panelist at many state and national conferences on technology, social studies curriculum, and leadership topics. He has provided professional development for IL ASCD (Association for Supervision and Curriculum Development) and is active in the ICSS (Illinois Council for Social Studies) and NSSLA (National Social Studies Leaders Association). He advocates that equity matters, not just globally but also locally, and that all students deserve equity and access in education and in life.

He has twenty-four years of experience in education, including time as a teacher in K–12 settings for both regular classrooms and alternative schools, as a social studies department chair, instructional technology coach, adjunct professor in social studies and instructional technology, and as a school and district administrator. Micah currently serves as the District Instructional Technology and Social Studies Coordinator at Maywood-Melrose Park-Broadview School District 89 near Chicago.

In addition to his book *AI Goes to School*, Micah is a contributing writer for the American Consortium for Equity in Education. He is also a Chicago Teach Plus Alum. Micah is a happy husband and father of four children in Chicago.

Dive into his website, micahminer.com, to explore his writings and articles for both peer-reviewed and non-peer-reviewed journals, professional development opportunities, and other valuable information.

Connect with Micah
website: micahminer.com
email: minerclass@gmail.com
X (Twitter): @minerclass
LinkedIn: linkedin.com/in/micah-j-miner

Acknowledgments

I would like to thank Times 10 Publications founder Mark Barnes and editors Regina Bell and Jennifer Jas, as well as the book designer Michelle M. White, who assisted in producing *AI Goes to School*. Without their interest in this topic and their confidence that I could assist educators who are grappling with this new and exciting technology, we couldn't have created this book to help teachers become better educators and students become more prepared for their futures.

Sneak Peek
Hacking Student Motivation

HACK 1

DESIGN AN INFORMATIVE GRADE BOOK

Communicate Progress and Growth Rather than Completion and Grades

I have a love-hate relationship with grades because I like seeing that I have all A's, but at the same time, even when you have a perfect 4.0, you are not happy . . .
I don't think teachers see how that affects a student's mental health.
— ANONYMOUS STUDENT ON A GRADING SURVEY

THE PROBLEM:
TRADITIONAL GRADES DON'T PROMOTE MEANINGFUL ENGAGEMENT

I still remember the exact moment I realized my grade book was absolutely meaningless. It was 2013, and I was finishing up the year at McLoughlin High School in Milton-Freewater, Oregon. This was before anyone trusted an online grade book enough for us to submit our final grades digitally. As such, I was walking down the hallway to the office with my grade book in hand, and as I flipped through the pages, I realized I knew nothing more about my students' learning than I would have known without them.

For context before we really dive in, see Image 1.1 for an idea of what my grade book looked like as I carried it down the hallway.

	QUIZ 1	UNIT NOTES	WORK-SHEET	QUIZ 2	REVIEW	UNIT TEST	FINAL GRADE
STUDENT A	7	10	5	8	10	23	84%
STUDENT B	4	5	0	3	10	27	65%
STUDENT C	8	10	5	8	10	19	80%

Image 1.1: Sample contents in my old grade book.

I taught mostly eleventh grade students at the time, and I pictured handing my grade book to their twelfth grade teacher and saying, "I want you to have this so that you know what your incoming students need to focus on." They would laugh, I would laugh, and then we would continue doing the same lessons without knowing why year after year.

That moment in the hallway, inside a hundred-year-old brick building, standing on an old carpet covered with stains, I made a decision. I decided I didn't want to be like that building, stuck in an antiquated system. I wanted to change, to renovate the way I assessed students, and to do it better. I dropped off the grade book, went back to my classroom, and started to figure out how to do it better.

I didn't have a classroom built for learning; I had a vending machine for grades—put an assignment in, get a grade out.

To start with, I had to pinpoint the problems before trying to solve them. I pulled up the backup copy of my grade book and stared at it for a long time, returning again and again to one very simple idea: the point of any form of academic records is to clearly communicate where a student is in their learning. The root of the problem is that my grade book wasn't communicating what I wanted it to. It fell short.

My epiphany about the meaninglessness of my grade book was that it focused on tasks, not learning. Ask any student what they need to do to improve their grade, and almost all of them will talk about the tasks and assignments they need to complete. Do students still need to complete certain tasks to prove evidence of learning? Yes, but that's not what I wanted students to solely focus on. The tasks, like quizzes and projects, were meant to be vehicles, the means to an end, and yet because of the way my grade book was set up, the tasks were the priority, the most prominent piece of the grade book connected to the final grade.

Essentially, I didn't have a classroom built for learning; I had a vending machine for grades—put an assignment in, get a grade out. I was creating grade-hungry monsters in my classroom who didn't even seem to recognize that learning was involved in any part of that process, and it showed. Each task was an island of performance, and students were skipping from each one, doing a task and moving on to the next seemingly disconnected task. Rarely did I get to talk about learning. Instead, I had conversations about points: "How do I get my grade up?" "How many points is this assignment worth?" I had to find a way to shift that dialogue, that mindset, so that we focused on learning. My challenge: How do I develop a grade book that centers the learning, not the tasks meant to support it?

Now, did these assignments provide me with *some* data? Absolutely. If a student struggled on a quiz, I knew to check in with that student. If a student didn't complete the notes, I knew we needed to have a conversation. If the whole class failed a test, I knew I had some reteaching to do.

However, there were two problems with this structure. First, I was still focused on tasks. Often, the way I responded to a student who failed a test was to have them retake the test. Missing notes? Come in and see me during an intervention time to get the notes.

Second, and most important, the data I had wasn't useful because it was overly cumbersome in identifying trends and patterns. For example, if the unit test covered multiple topics, how was I supposed to know which topic specifically needed my attention and more class time? If I were going to pull out a small group for an intervention, how was I supposed to quickly identify which students needed support in which topics if I were taking all that information and combining it into a single score for "test" in the grade book?

I had a lot of data but not a lot of information. By this, I mean that I had a lot of numbers and nowhere to go with them. One of the most valuable efforts we can make for our students is to help them see their success and growth. My grade book didn't show that.

My goal was to find a way to organize that information so it was quick and easy to understand what needed to happen and for whom.

It was like some weird game of Twister, where each skill was awkwardly intertwined with all the other skills in that unit. I wanted students to be able to look at the record of their learning and easily be able to tell me where they were growing and where they were stuck without having to untwist their grading data to do it. Often, because we covered multiple standards in a unit, one assignment in the grade book would be about one skill, and then the next assignment would be about a different skill. As a result, when you looked through the grade book, it wasn't a record of growth about a specific skill but rather a smattering of concepts that were stepping over each other. I needed to make it quick and easy to identify trends in their learning.

THE HACK:
DESIGN AN INFORMATIVE GRADE BOOK

Standards-based grading in and of itself is not revolutionary. It does not guarantee that assessment will become meaningful in your classroom, that your classroom will be a more equitable place, and that your students will become highly motivated learners.

Standards-based grading does one simple and powerful job: it opens doors to the type of classroom where students understand how to be active, motivated participants in their learning process. Once those doors are open, however, the work remains to be done in terms of pedagogical approaches to the way we design learning and assessments. A standards-based approach to assessment, when paired with an increase in student ownership in the learning process, was the doorway to a richer learning environment in my classroom.

Instead of asking, "What do I want my students to do?" it forced me to start thinking, "What do I want my students to know?"

Standards-based grading is a natural starting point, and it's an important one because it forces a shift in the instruction and assessment in the classroom to focus on specific standards and goals. For me, it helped me change where I start planning. Instead of asking, "What do I want my students to do?" it forced me to start thinking, "What do I want my students to know?" When we start with that question, we create more freedom, both in our teaching and in how students can experience their learning. When I start by creating what I want students to *do*, I'm narrowing the room for creativity, choice, and individuality, and it often means I began by building an assessment. When I shifted to focus on the learning first, I realized that I had opportunities for students to exert some control over how they learned the content and how they demonstrated their learning.

This autonomy for students, the ability to have some control over an experience, is a huge element of motivation. For example, when I was a kid, one of my jobs was to mow the lawn. I was told to do it. I hated it, absolutely hated it. It was like pulling teeth to get me to do it. As an adult with my own house and lawn, now I find myself in full-blown dad-mode, getting excited to get out and work in the yard. Did the task change? Did the person involved change? No, it is still me mowing the lawn. The difference? I am in control of it, and as a result, I take more pride in it. It is meaningful to me because I can choose if, when, and how to do it.

This is just one of the doors that can be opened by standards-based assessment and learning: the ability to increase the autonomy that students experience and to create an avenue for students to truly see their growth. When I was focused on isolated tasks in my grade book, growth was difficult to spot. Yes, there was an increase in quiz scores, but what did that mean about the learning? Additionally, growth in a quiz connects to an artificial goal. That quiz is arbitrary, but when the growth is visible in terms of the learning the student is engaged in, the knowledge is building inside their brain. That ability to see growth is a huge factor in motivation. When we see we're growing, we believe we have the capacity to be successful in later attempts, and when we believe that, we have a solid foundation for motivation to grow.

Seeing self-growth communicates to students that no matter where they start, they have the potential to be successful. Here's an example to illustrate this: In a traditional grade book, where the final grade is a simple average of the attempts over time, a student who scores low on the first attempt will always have a lower average score than someone who came in with a better understanding of the concept. Even if those two students end up performing at equal levels in later attempts to demonstrate their learning, if we average scores over time, like my grade book did at the beginning of my career, we are telling students, "Where you come from will dictate how far you can go." Obviously, we would never say that outright to a student, but grading is a form of communication, and if we are holding students accountable for their early attempts at learning without the opportunity for better subsequent attempts, that's the message we are communicating.

These two elements of motivation, autonomy and visible growth, come from a re-prioritization of the grade book. For me, this meant that my headers in my grade book were no longer labeled as tasks, but rather, those headers were the learning students engaged in. Underneath that was a record of how they performed on those skills over time. This allowed me to both see the growth and to value it when it came time to determine a final score for each skill. See Image 1.2.

	SKILL			
	Attempt 1	Attempt 2	Attempt 3	Current
STUDENT A				
STUDENT B				
STUDENT C				

Image 1.2: My current learning-focused grade book.

Your grade book redesign can look countless ways, but they all start with a simple question: "How does my grade book communicate that the most important goal in the classroom is learning and growth?" It was this question that helped me redesign my grade book so that it built motivation instead of hindered it.

While that question is complex and may require major changes, which are detailed step-by-step in the full implementation section later, simply asking that question turned out to be the hack I didn't realize my whole classroom needed.

More from Times 10 Publications

Hacking School Discipline
9 Ways to Create a Culture of Empathy & Responsibility Using Restorative Justice
By Nathan Maynard and Brad Weinstein

Reviewers proclaimed this original *Hacking School Discipline* book and *Washington Post* bestseller to be "maybe the most important book a teacher can read, a must for all educators, fabulous, a game-changer!" Teachers and presenters Maynard and Weinstein demonstrate how to eliminate punishment and build a culture of responsible students and independent learners at the classroom level. Twenty-one straight months at #1 on Amazon, *Hacking School Discipline* disrupted education in a big way.

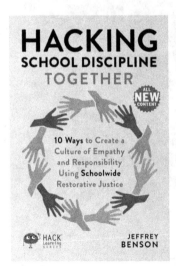

Hacking School Discipline Together
10 Ways to Create a Culture of Empathy and Responsibility Using Schoolwide Restorative Justice
By Jeffrey Benson

Hacking School Discipline Together is the sequel to *Hacking School Discipline*. This book, with all new content, goes beyond the classroom level and helps all administrators, teachers, and staff members create a culture of responsible students at the schoolwide and systemwide levels. Veteran educator Jeffrey Benson provides a road map to reduce stress around discipline and create staff unity, compassion, and consistency.

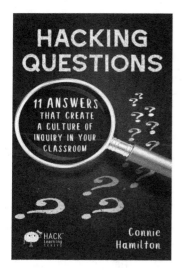

Hacking Questions
11 Answers that Create a Culture of Inquiry in Your Classroom
By Connie Hamilton

Questions are the driving force of learning, and teachers have questions about how to engage students with the art of questioning. *Hacking Questions* digs into framing, delivering, and maximizing questions to keep students engaged in learning. Known in education circles as the "Questioning Guru," Hamilton shows teachers of all subjects and grades how to ask the questions that deliver reflection, metacognition, and real learning.

Hacking Deficit Thinking
8 Reframes That Will Change the Way You Think about Strength-Based Practices and Equity in Schools
By Byron McClure and Kelsie Reed

Too many teachers are focused on what's wrong with their students instead of what's strong. This focus on weakness is a pervasive, powerful judgment that continues to harm students long after they leave school. It's time for educators to reframe teaching and learning. McClure and Reed show how to unlearn student blame and reframe thinking to focus on students' strengths, benefitting them for life.

Hacking Life After 50
10 Ways to Beat Father Time and Live a Long, Healthy, Joy-Filled Life
By James Sturtevant and Mark Barnes

After-50s life can be overwhelming if people think their best years are in the past. *Hacking Life After 50* shares 10 strategies you can use today to live a long, happy, joy-filled life. Sturtevant and Barnes show how to create purpose in life, build momentum regardless of age, master meal planning, reclaim muscle, sleep better than ever, and discover simple acts that promote healthy, happy living. Make your life's Act II the best it can be.

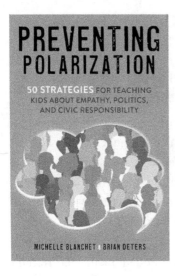

Preventing Polarization
50 Strategies for Teaching Kids about Empathy, Politics, and Civic Responsibility
By Michelle Blanchet and Brian Deters

In an era that has become incredibly polarized politically and socially, we can help our students learn to come together despite differences and become active and engaged citizens. A one-off civics course is not enough. Learn basic strategies to create experiences that help students break down barriers through activities and role playing. Let's show our students how to make a difference, minimize conflict, and build accord.

TIMES 10 PUBLICATIONS provides practical solutions that busy educators can read today and use tomorrow. We bring you content from experienced teachers and leaders, and we share it through books, podcasts, webinars, articles, events, and ongoing conversations on social media. Our books and materials help turn practice into action. Stay in touch with us at 10Publications.com and follow our updates on X @10Publications and #Times10News.

www.ingramcontent.com/pod-product-compliance
Lightning Source LLC
LaVergne TN
LVHW022307060326
832902LV00020B/3315